A WORLD OF POSSIBILITY

A WORLD OF POSSIBILITY

An Autobiography

BARNEY A. EBSWORTH

HUNTS POINT PUBLISHING
HUNTS POINT, WA

© 2012 Barney A. Ebsworth

Published by
Hunts Point Publishing
Hunts Point, WA

Publisher's Cataloging-in-Publication Data
Ebsworth, Barney A.

       A world of possibility : an autobiography / Barney A.
       Ebsworth. – Hunts Point, WA : Hunts Point Pub., 2012.

       p. ; cm.

       ISBN13: 978-0-9860241-0-8

       1. Ebsworth, Barney A. 2. Businessmen—United States—
       Biography. I. Title.

       HC102.5.E27 A3 2012
       338.092—dc23   2012948365

Project coordination by Jenkins Group, Inc.
www.BookPublishing.com

Interior design by Brooke Camfield

Printed in the United States of America
16   15   14   13   12   •   5   4   3   2   1

Dedication

To Mom, Dad, and Christiane

Contents

Chapter One
HEAD OF THE FAMILY 1

Chapter Two
$12,000 A YEAR 15

Chapter Three
ARMY DAYS 27

Chapter Four
FALLING FOR FRANCE 37

Chapter Five
THE TRAVEL BUSINESS 47

Chapter Six
INTRAV 67

Chapter Seven
MAKING HISTORY 77

Chapter Eight
CRUISING 101

Chapter Nine
BRINGING THE MUSEUM HOME   127

Chapter Ten
GEORGIA O'KEEFFE   139

Chapter Eleven
THE EXPERIENCE   159

Chapter Twelve
RETIREMENT   173

AFTERWORD   189

Chapter One

HEAD OF THE FAMILY

I am a very lucky man. I have had the kind of wonderful life that many people dream about—I've traveled the world many times over, befriended celebrities, run several successful businesses that ensured I haven't had to worry about money, fathered a terrific daughter and become a grandfather, and have dedicated a good portion of my life to my passion of collecting art. But this life didn't spring forth from nowhere. It started with the best possible foundation: two loving parents.

My father, Alec W. Ebsworth, started out with the most auspicious beginning an Englishman can have. He was born in Windsor Castle.

His father was a Grenadier Guard, one of the five regiments of the British army that form the Queen's Foot Guards. He commanded the guards at Windsor Castle, and he and my grandmother lived there—the largest occupied castle in the world and official residence of the queen. The castle was 800 years old by then and run with such precision that an official measuring stick was used to calculate the distance from each chair to each table.

"How glamorous!" people usually say when I tell them this, and I'm tempted to leave it at that, but in the interest of honesty, I'll disclose that they lived in the casements, which is a fancy word for cells. Cold stone must have made it a terrible place to live, but still, my dad was born in the castle's infirmary right across from St. George's Chapel.

On the other side of the family, my maternal grandfather and namesake had a remarkable history of his own. I seemingly inherited his entrepreneurial spirit in addition to his name. He ran the passenger side of St. Louis Union Station when it opened in 1892. His ticket agents wrote train tickets, and one of them complained of feeling overburdened: "People come to the office wanting to know all about St. Louis, and we don't have time to write tickets."

This was the impetus for my grandfather to start the first tourist information bureau in the United States. He built it just so he could direct people somewhere away from his ticket agents when they wanted to ask questions about the city.

Shortly thereafter, it was announced that the World's Fair was coming to St. Louis in 1904. Could the employees at the information kiosk handle the extra traffic? They were dubious. "We're going to be swamped!" they told him. And they were right, of course. The title "the World's Fair" was accurate in more ways than one: not only would displays of cultural artifacts and technological advances be presented from all over the world but also the world was coming to St. Louis. Nearly 20 million people made the trip, with an average daily attendance of 100,000. That was a rather significant influx of bewildered tourists roaming around the city in search of guidance.

In response to the expected demand, my grandfather wrote the first-known guidebook to a city in the United States. The cover displayed his photo—he was bald by the time he was 29—and a big question mark. The title was *Ask Barney about St. Louis*. He figured this would move people through the information bureau faster and keep the place orderly.

When people ask me today about the genesis of my interest in the travel industry, I have to wonder whether my family background played a role. Did it come from my maternal or paternal side of the family? One grandfather living in Windsor Castle, the other starting a tourism information bureau and writing a travel guidebook—maybe it came from both sides.

My parents aren't the most likely couple; after all, my father's family tree had its roots in England, and my mother was from St. Louis. When my father was young, his father was a brigadier general in the British army and fought in France in World War I. He had been wounded twice in the Boer War (1898–1899). I had surmised that if you were wounded back then, you had little chance of survival because of the poor state of medicine. After all, you could die from stepping on a rusty nail. Yet he not only survived but also lived to fight in World War I, where he was wounded twice more. He received the Military Cross, the second-highest award for valor in the British army (second only to the Victorian Cross). Then, six weeks shy of the end of the war, he was shot again and killed.

That was very unfortunate for his family but not as unfortunate for me, because if he had not been killed, I almost certainly never would have been born.

When my grandfather left for war, my dad was 10 years old, with two younger siblings and a third on the way. They were a military family run with strict discipline. I don't believe my dad had much of a childhood even before the war, but certainly the time was a stressful one for him when his father was gone.

My fantasy has always been that before my grandfather left, he patted my dad on the head and said, "Alec, you're the head of the family now."

When my grandfather was killed, that made my father's role permanent. My dad was just 14, and now he had a younger brother and two younger sisters. The weighty sense of responsibility got to him, and he announced to his family that he wanted to emigrate to the United States.

"Finish high school first," his mother told him. "Then spend one year in Cambridge. After that, you can make up your mind about whether to go."

So that's exactly what he did. He finished his one year in Cambridge and then left for St. Louis. Why St. Louis? His maternal grandmother, whom he called Gran, was married to a sea captain who vanished at sea around India before the turn of the century. So she remarried William Ailen, a master potter from the English Midlands. In 1902, William was brought to St. Louis to make fancy terra cotta for the World's Fair, a celebration of the Louisiana Purchase's one-hundredth anniversary.

Sixty-two nations and 43 states were represented there. After the fair was over, they stayed—so my father had a grandmother in the States whom he hadn't met. That's how he ended up in St. Louis and staying with Gran for a while.

I'm not sure whether he knew what he was in for; Gran was one tough cookie. Everyone was scared to death of her, adults and kids alike. You had to watch your mouth around her or risk her wrath, so when I met her later, I tried to keep my mouth shut.

My mom, on the other hand, had been born in St. Louis and was the baby of the family. After her father left the railroad, he became president of the St. Louis Railway Company, which was really a streetcar and bus company. What this meant to my mother, more than anything, was that he was a big mucky-muck in the Mysterious Order of the Veiled Prophet.

The Veiled Prophet is a charitable organization started in 1878 to promote St. Louis. Each year, it orchestrates several events, including balls and fairs, but the biggest of its attractions was the annual parade, and the reason my grandfather was important to the group was that it ran the parade over the streetcar tracks. With more than a dozen elaborate floats, hundreds of costumed participants, debutantes practicing their waves, and a marching band competition, the parade rivals Mardi Gras. My mother loved to take part in Veiled Prophet balls and events; I think she grew up with a bit of a delusion of grandeur because of this. She was the economy version of Scarlett O'Hara.

Her father had supposedly been the sergeant at arms of a Democratic National Convention in the 1890s, and then he switched and became a Republican and was the sergeant at arms of a Republican National Convention. My mother was Republican because her father was.

She was working at the St. Louis Railway Company when my dad was hired there, which is how they met. He was debonair and charming; she was cute and cuddly. To top it off, my father was super liberal, so they politically nullified each other.

I have no idea how he proposed, but knowing my dad, he didn't hire a band and shoot off fireworks and make a big production out of it. They were married in March of 1933, and on July 14, 1934, my twin sister and I were born, right in the middle of the Depression. It was 105 degrees that day when my mother was in labor, and in those days, the men didn't stay in the room while the women gave birth. They waited out in the hall for the groaning and unpleasantries to be over. So at 10:30 in the morning, a nurse came out and said, "Mr. Ebsworth, the first one is a girl."

"The *first one*?" he said. Evidently, they had no idea they were having more than one. The famous Dionne quintuplets had just been born that May and made headlines, so he began to panic, imagining five babies were about to be placed in his unprepared arms.

Luckily, it was just one more: me. But I didn't make my appearance until 2:30 that afternoon. All those hours in labor with no air conditioning. If that doesn't make you love your mother, I don't know what does.

On our birth certificates, it says, "Mother's occupation: Housewife. Father's occupation: Unemployed." We're worried about the 9 percent unemployment rate now, but then, it was 25 percent. My father never finished college and worked mostly clerical jobs, so it was lucky that my mother's father had done well and was willing to help them. My mother's bachelorette sister, Aunt Jean, also lived with us about half the time, and she worked at the post office and helped pay the bills.

The house, however, was always Dad's castle. He was the more dominant one in the household, and my mother capitulated to his wishes. I saw her argue with him only once in my entire childhood. Maybe once and a half. The match wasn't an unhealthy one, though, because my father's dominance was good spirited.

My sister, Muriel, failed to pick up my mother's submissive gene. It was quickly apparent that my sister wasn't the girly-girl type. She wasn't big, but she was scrappy. Twin girls lived in the apartment across from us, and when we were five and they were six, their mother came by and said, "I'm going to the store with the girls. Would the twins like to come with us?"

"That's very nice," my mother said, and she sent us off with her.

The girls were in the backseat when we got to the car. A fight ensued about who would get the window seats. My sister ended up at the window, and the two six-year-old girls beat the hell out of me. I guess I was an easier target; my sister was just intimidating. She'd stick her nose out and people would back down. She didn't actually fight much, but she was a tomboy who just didn't take nonsense from anybody.

Five days before Christmas that same year, my mother had gone shopping and my dad was supposed to be watching us, but he had fallen asleep on the sofa. To occupy us, I cut all of my twin sister's hair off. Now, she was a very powerful force, so she must have been in full agreement or I never would have done it. I still remember the look on my mother's face when she walked in. *Aghast.*

We moved to Kingshighway when I was 12, the downstairs of a two-story flat. It had white limestone steps that we were supposed to scrub on Saturdays and a porch out front. The living room was average size, but the bedroom Muriel and I shared was scarcely big enough for our bunk beds. There was just enough room to hit the floor when you climbed down from the top bunk. When our Aunt Jean stayed with us, she slept on a convertible sofa bed. It was definitely . . . cozy. I didn't really mind, though.

I can remember getting into only two fights with Muriel. The first was during a game of softball. She was the batter, and I was the catcher, and she let go of the bat that hit me in the stomach. The other time, I lunged at her, and she sidestepped, and I hit a concrete wall. Those were the last times I messed with Muriel.

When I was at my twenty-fifth class reunion, I remember running into the guy who was once the grade school bully. Now he was a CPA.

"You and I are the same size now," I said, grabbing his tie. "You were the bully, but I'm going to get you now."

"Bully? I wasn't the bully," he said.

"Yes, you were. Maybe other guys, too, but you were the real bully."

"No, there's someone else in class who always terrorized me."

"Who?"

"Your twin sister."

I stopped for a moment. I wasn't quite expecting that.

"So that's why you never picked on me," I said. "You beat on everyone else in class, but you left me alone."

"Right. I was afraid your sister would pound on me if I touched you."

I hadn't even realized that I had a protector in school. It's a really good thing that she was a girl, though, because I'm afraid that if she'd been a boy, one of us would not have survived our youth. We were both extremely competitive, but I didn't feel as threatened by her accomplishments because she was a girl and therefore on a different playing field.

As for me, I was an excellent student, with particular interest in history and geography. I also collected stamps and coins. Muriel was a very good student and an exceptional athlete as well.

Our parents were terrific parents—they were just *there* for us. Mom was everything a mom should be, and Dad was everything a dad should be. She was more affectionate; he was more of a cheerleader. She was everybody's mother. He was the buttoned-up model of a perfect Englishman, with the accompanying difficulty in expressing emotions. He didn't say he loved me, but that didn't matter because I felt it all the time in his actions. I guess I've inherited some of that, too. I can't really imagine myself saying "I love you" to my sister, but I do. I think she's great.

My dad didn't verbalize his pride in me when I brought home a perfect report card; it was just expected. It was just like in bowling—according to his view, you were supposed to bowl a 300 game every time, and when you bowled less than that, you needed to improve. I expect that if I ever came home and said, "Dad! I bowled a 300 game today," he would have responded, "How about the other two games?" But I still knew that he was proud, and I knew that he would do anything for us. He became a scout leader when I was in the Boy Scouts, and he showed up at our sports.

My mother cooked, though not very well. My dad's idea of cooking was just to pour sauce over everything. We certainly didn't live in a gourmet household. We visited local museums a couple of times, but my parents weren't into art or theater. That was fine with me because, like most kids my age, I would have much rather played baseball than gone to some old museum, anyway. The first time I can remember being talked into going to a museum was when the St. Louis Art Museum had a 3,000-year-old mummy with an exposed brown toe on display. Curiosity dictated that I had to see the mummy, but I also remember having nightmares about it coming to get me at night.

Aunt Jean took us to church on Sundays, and I acquiesced just to be dutiful. I don't remember caring very much about church then, but it was something I was supposed to do.

The only time I remember my dad going to church was in February of 1952 for King George VI's memorial service. It seemed strange to me that my father wanted to attend this service, considering he'd been in the United States during all of George VI's reign. At the time, I thought, "I guess he's a loyal Englishman." When the movie *The King's Speech* debuted in 2010,

I finally understood: George VI was a stutterer, and so was my father. It was something that was very embarrassing to him. He felt a kinship with George VI that he never voiced. Life's funny that way—you just keep peeling back layers until you understand people better, both yourself and others.

I rarely crossed my parents, and don't think I ever gave them reason to discipline me beyond the age of eight. I also don't remember ever being spanked, though I'm sure they probably gave me a few swats when I was very young. For the most part, I was a good kid who appreciated that he had a wonderful family.

Muriel and I were the outgoing youngsters who organized all the neighborhood sports. The fact that Muriel was a girl didn't matter, and we mostly played "boys' sports." I'd still pick her over most boys.

We'd gather up six or seven kids and go to the alley to play a makeshift baseball game and hope that nobody would hit a ball and break someone's window. When we heard the sound of breaking glass, everybody had to take off. I lost count of how many times that happened.

There was less chance of us breaking windows when we played corkball—a sport that originated in St. Louis. Corkballs were smaller and softer than regular baseballs, and the bats were thin. But since we didn't have any money, a lot of the time we just played with sawed-off broomsticks and bottle caps.

Some days, we went across to the school yard to play baseball, and we broke a lot of windows there, too. We spent much of our time outdoors—not "nature" outdoors but urban outdoors. As long as the schoolwork was done, our parents were happy to have us occupied and out of their hair. The house was quiet, unlike when I was home practicing the violin, which I played abysmally for five years. (My sister played it longer and much better.) But while we were out playing, my dad had time to read.

He was an avid reader, reading just about every science fiction and mystery novel that came down the pike, as well as books about the World Wars. Dad was lucky enough to have been too young to get drafted for World War I and too old to get drafted for World War II, but he sure was interested in reading about both of them. When I picture him now, I see him with a moustache, glasses, a pipe, and a book in his hands.

I became an avid reader as well. Friends of mine tell me I could write my own book about World War II.

"How did you learn so much about it?" they'll ask.

"I grew up reading the newspaper," I say. I began reading the newspaper every afternoon when I was about eight years old. I knew that if we lost this war, our lives were going to be a lot different, so I paid attention.

Partly because my dad was English and I still had family in England whom I'd never met and partly because of reading newspapers and books, I developed an interest in the world outside my hometown. The world was big, to be sure, and there was so much I wanted to explore someday.

My school didn't have any money, so we didn't get to take a spring break trip to Washington, D.C., like almost all the other schools did. And our family didn't have any money, either, so we didn't do much traveling beyond short car trips. I can remember one trip when I was about five to Lake Taneycomo, near Branson, Missouri. It was a town of around 1,200 people at the time; now it's a major tourist destination that draws more people each summer than Disney World and Las Vegas. We were in bed at about 9:00 with the windows open one night when I heard beautiful music coming from the other side of the lake—and it turned out to be Glenn Miller playing "Moonlight Serenade." When I hear it now, it brings back great memories.

We also stayed about 90 miles out of St. Louis at Fox Springs Lodge two or three times, and that was about it, except for the times we went to Chicago to play cricket during the Fourth of July weekend. Sometimes we stayed in a dormitory and sometimes in a hotel, which was very impressive to me—a big-city hotel!

But the trips I really dreamed about were more elaborate than that . . . my favorite books were travel narratives, such as Richard Halliburton's *The Royal Road to Romance*, about his adventures all over the world. He called himself a "horizon chaser," and I identified with that. I was always interested in seeing what was over the next hill.

"One day," I thought, "I'm going to go *everywhere*."

And you know what? I did.

Chapter Two

$12,000 A YEAR

When I was 12 years old in 1946, I had two uncles whom I greatly admired. My mother's brother-in-law Cliff started in newspaper sales but became an advertising executive, and my mother's only brother, Ed, was the general manager of Westinghouse Air Brake Company. Westinghouse manufactured air brakes for railroad cars.

These two uncles each made $12,000 a year, and they both owned their own houses and cars, so I extrapolated that if you wanted to be successful, that's what you had to earn. They were the standards for me, representing a financial security that we did not have. In terms of today's economy, they were earning about the income of midlevel executives.

Dad, who didn't have a college degree, probably made $5,000 a year or less working clerical jobs. Our money situation was always very tenuous, and as a child, I worried that we were going to be separated when the money ran out. Twice, my father lost his job. I don't believe he ever had more than $100 in the bank.

On holidays, we'd generally go to Uncle Ed's house, because his was the biggest house and the biggest family. My cousins on my mother's side were 10 years older than we were, so as they grew up and moved away, we spent more time with my dad's side of the family. Two years after my dad came to America, he brought over his younger brother, Ernie, and then about six years later, they brought their sister Edith. Their other sister, Muriel, stayed in England with their mother and never came over.

The three who emigrated had different accents—my dad had a good British accent, my uncle sounded like he was from Boston, and my Aunt Edith sounded like she was right off the boat—"pip, pip, cheerio, rather" and all that. Their accents seemed to fit their jobs; my white-collar dad liked sounding like a British gentleman, my uncle became a supply manager for an industrial company and liked being more Americanized, and my aunt worked as head seamstress at Saks, where I imagine her accent gave her some prestige.

I remember really hurting my father's feelings once, and that was when I was an adult and describing my childhood to someone with my father standing nearby. I said, "We grew up poor," and I saw my dad's face fall. I realized in that moment that I'd just wounded his pride severely, which wasn't my intention, and that maybe he didn't see us that way. Maybe "poor" should be reserved for those who have no food or shelter—we had those. We always had enough food, and we had our little flat. Although we didn't have a car, we always lived close to a bus line.

I'm sure my father characterized himself as a failure. He was the eldest son, and between the fact that he stuttered and the fact that he never had an impressive career or earned a significant salary, he didn't think much of himself. I, on the other hand, thought the world of him.

I worried more than a child probably should about what could happen to us. It made me work harder in school because, even then, I understood that education was the key to a better future. Early on, signs indicated I would be an entrepreneur, from my lemonade stands to the terra cotta Indians I made using molds. Although I wasn't sure what kind of business I wanted to go into, I knew I wanted to be my own boss. If I worked hard enough, maybe I could be like my uncles and make enough money to own my own home and support a family.

Uncle Cliff came to our house one day and said, "I got the Lee account in Kansas City, Missouri!" The company was known mostly for its jelly, but it also made Lee blue jeans. So he said to me, "Barney, I've been hired to help them do their marketing. They make great blue jeans, but they don't sell. Levi is the hottest thing going. How come?"

I said, "Well, what kids love about Levi's are the little rivets and the red Levi tag and the leather patch in the back."

"So what do you suggest?" he asked.

"I suggest you do that with Lee. You need a logo and a leather patch and some rivets."

He made a logo in blue and yellow and put on a leather patch. At 12 years old, I made that company with that advice. Lee has been making money with those same jeans for more than 60 years.

This kind of "magic touch" followed me throughout life, where I achieved success seemingly easier than my peers. I earned Eagle Scout status as quickly as one can do it. My dad was very concerned with my becoming the youngest Eagle Scout at age 14. He said, "The problem with getting it so early is that you go from being a Boy Scout to being a girl scout."

He was about right. My first date was at around 15 years old, when I took out a girl named Barbara from Sunday school. Her family had a bakery in town. My dad had to drive me to the date.

When I say that my dad was right there with me in life, I mean it literally: my dad became an Eagle Scout along with me.

Dad was the assistant scoutmaster. Not only did that add to his credentials as a great dad but also it allowed him to have a belated childhood.

He is the first person known to have achieved both King's Scout in England and Eagle Scout in the United States—King's Scout being the British equivalent. My dad received his badge from the founder of the Boy Scout movement, Lord Robert Baden-Powell. Since 1953, when Queen Elizabeth II took over the throne, the title has been called Queen's Scout instead.

The Philmont Scout Ranch in Cimarron, New Mexico, opened in 1947 as the national training center for Boy Scouts, and I went with the first group of Scouts from St. Louis about a year later. We had to take a Greyhound bus all night to get there, and it was thrilling. We made a stop in Dodge City, Kansas, at 4 a.m. so they could clean the bus. I remember getting off the bus and looking all around, hoping I'd see the sheriff stroll by in a cowboy hat.

I got five more merit badges after becoming an Eagle Scout, which meant I got an extra palm. Beyond that, I moved onto other pursuits and goals.

I had been a mostly A and sometimes B student until I realized that I'd need straight As to earn a college scholarship. From my junior year in high school all the way through college, I made straight As and never once took a sick day. The only subject that was arduous for me was calculus; even though I got an A, I couldn't tell you anything I learned two weeks after the final exam. What I'd truly aced was short-term memorization.

We were lucky in those days that you didn't really have to do your homework at home. I had two study halls, and I could get all my work done in that time, which meant that my time after school really was free time. Most of my after-school hours were spent on sports: cross-country in fall and track in spring.

Track was more my style, and that's what turned out to be "my" sport. I was on the B team my freshman year and then moved up to varsity in my sophomore year. Senior year, I was the city sprint champion in the 100, 220, and 440. I was also captain of the cross-country team even though I hated distance running. I hated every two miles I ran, but I persevered. My dad attended every meet.

Once I started taking track seriously, I gave myself a bedtime of 9:00. I figured that if eight hours of sleep per night were good, then 10 hours would give me the extra competitive edge.

The University of Missouri offered me a track scholarship. A student could receive only four types of scholarships at the time, and over the course of my college years, I got them all: freshman, academic, athletic, and need based. I went to the University of Missouri because it gave me the most scholarship money. My sister wanted to teach in an elementary school, so she went to a city college that trained teachers.

Although I had scholarship money, it wasn't a full ride, so I took on odd jobs and worked my way through college.

My freshman roommate was a fellow I went to high school with, and every morning, he'd look at himself in the mirror and say, "Ugly, ugly, ugly!" The poor guy wasn't even that bad looking . . . at least until he got into a car accident and came back with a 10-inch gash across his face. That didn't help. Friends of his would visit sometimes, but I still studied even when he had company. One time he had a fight with the school's star basketball player over a Nazi knife, and they crashed all over the room. "Someone's going to get hurt," I thought . . . but I kept studying anyway. No one died.

The guys in my dorm were a bunch of characters. One student down the hall had a Model T Ford in perfect condition, and when he flew home for the holidays, the guys who stayed on campus disassembled his car, carried it inside, and reassembled it in the middle of his dorm room. Quite a sight.

Rarely did I take part in any of these shenanigans, though—I was too serious. I had arrived at college with Olympic dreams in my head, which quickly came crashing down when I saw the level of competition against which I was now competing. In the NCAA finals, I ran 9.6 seconds in the 100-yard dash and came in dead last. When you run 9.6 and see seven rear ends in front of you, even though the world record is 9.3, you know there's not much future left for you in the sport.

We were all white and skinny, and we were allowed to do push-ups and sit-ups but no weight lifting or the coach would expel us from the team. Nowadays, most track stars are big, muscular African American guys. I doubt a white guy has been in the finals in the past 10 years. It's not that there were no African American track stars at that time—after all, Ralph Peacock ran at Penn State in the 1920s, and Jesse Owens ran at Ohio State in the 1930s—it was just a freak year. At other points, I was the only white guy in a race, as in the 100-yard invitational in East St. Louis, where I set the record. We were running at night.

"The only reason you won is that you're the only one they could see in the dark," my dad said.

Thanks, Dad.

My coach was brutal. I spent all of homecoming weekend in the hospital while I was being treated for dehydration from an intestinal virus. I still felt terrible when I got out but went to track practice on Monday. The coach knew that the students on the team had just visited me in the hospital, but he took no mercy— he had me run two quarter-mile time trials while I struggled just to stay upright.

The NCAA had a rule that you couldn't run varsity in your freshman year, so I lettered in my second year. I came home and said, "Dad, your son is a varsity hero."

My sister lettered 16 times in her first two years.

Her achievements were a little bit humbling. She did eight sports per year, two at a time. One time in the jock hall at school, I read aloud a letter from home in which my mother told me that my sister had been injured. She was in the ninth inning of her softball game, and she was on third base, with a score of 0-0. She tried to steal home, slid, and broke her arm.

A big football player called out, "Well, was she safe or not?"

"I don't know," I said. "My mother didn't say."

He came over, picked me up by the back of my shirt, and took me to the phone. "Call her and find out."

I called. She was safe. The guy put me down.

My sister and I had similar dispositions; sports suited our competitive natures. No matter what I was doing, I wanted to be the best at it. I never did come close to my Olympic dreams, but I do think I went as far as my talent would allow me. The furthest I got was when I made it to the finals of the NCAA 100-yard dash and finished eighth. I probably had the determination of an Olympic runner, and I had good talent but not at that level. You need to have both great determination and great talent.

In my sophomore year of college, I convinced two buddies to take a daring trip with me. Richard Halliburton had written about climbing Mt. Fuji at night so he could watch the sunrise at the top of the mountain. I fancied following in Halliburton's footsteps, so I talked my friends into driving to Colorado and climbing Pikes Peak at night to watch the sunrise from the top of the mountain.

That night was hot, and we were wearing shorts and short-sleeved shirts. Despite a fine start, after a couple of hours, we were hopelessly lost on the mountain. What was the path, and what was the dry creek bed? At 2 a.m., after we'd been lost for three hours, we stumbled onto the cog railway tracks. A big sign said, "Keep off the tracks. Trespassers will be prosecuted."

Here's the difference between us: my friend Larry, who became a doctor, said, "We can't go up there. It wouldn't be sporting."

My other buddy, who would work for Social Security and was afraid of his own shadow, said, "We can't go up there. We'll be arrested for trespassing."

And then I—the entrepreneur—said, "I don't know about you, but I'm going up those railroad tracks. They go to the top."

We followed the tracks all the way up. We knew workers stayed up there all tourist season. The weather at the top of the mountain wasn't exactly like the weather at the bottom—now it was below freezing, with wind whipping our faces.

"Try knocking on that door. See whether they'll let us in," I said, but it was futile. With the loud 40-mile-per-hour winds in the middle of the night, no one could hear us. We couldn't raise anyone.

But then salvation arrived in the form of an eight-hole outhouse.

"Look over there!" I said, and we rushed into the outhouse. It had a heater, so it was at least warm, but you can imagine the putrid stench. I sat against the wall on the dirt floor and fell asleep, waking up in the same position. We slept there all night—filthy and smelly—and I had a terrible altitude headache. And I was climbing in, of all things, white bucks. We got to see the sunrise, but it didn't seem as glorious as in Halliburton's book. I suppose that's because he hadn't just spent a night in an outhouse.

Combining the hours I spent in class, studying, running track, and working, I was active at least 80 hours per week without any regular days off. I gave myself Saturday nights off, and I attended church on Sunday mornings mostly out of habit and a sense of obligation, and I went out to dinner on Sunday nights because everything on campus was closed.

Most summers, I worked two jobs, except for the summer I worked three. On Fridays, I worked at an ammunition factory from 7 a.m. until 4 p.m. and then rode the bus to Kroger bakery and loaded bakery trucks from 5 p.m. to 2 a.m. Then I went home and tried to get a few hours of sleep before selling clothes at a department store from 9 a.m. to 5 p.m. the next day. It was character building. I made straight As in school but almost made myself daft in the process.

After two years at Mizzou, I felt overloaded and burned out. I didn't like the pressure of my track scholarship; it was such a fierce level of competition, and it felt like a job. So when Washington University in St. Louis offered me an academic scholarship, I jumped at the chance. No track scholarship this time, which meant that I could do it just for fun again.

I transferred to Washington University's business school in St. Louis in time for my junior year and moved back home with my parents. Things were looking up a bit for them; my father had bought his first car, a used powder blue two-door Oldsmobile with fancy exhaust pipes. One day, he got pulled over for speeding, and the police officer came to the window and said, "Where do you think you're going, Hot Rod?"

My dad was the last person on earth you'd call "Hot Rod." We got a good laugh out of that.

Washington University was a better fit for me. The professors had more real-world business experience, and I was able to regain my status as a track star. The level of competition was lower, so I got to win again.

Toward the end of my senior year, I was running out of steam. Because of my grades, I gained entrance to a program that combined undergrad business courses with the beginning of law school. The draft was on, which meant that I would be forced into the military at some point after school was over. My plan was to go to law school, but I felt some uncertainty about that, so I thought, "Why don't I just go into the army and get it done, and by the time I get back, I'll have figured out whether I want to be in law school?"

I didn't want to settle into a new career or have a family and then find myself yanked out of it on someone else's terms. I wanted to be orderly about my affairs. Signing up voluntarily gave me a measure of control over when I'd go in and when I'd get out.

I had just received a letter from the dean saying I had achieved straight As again and had ranked number one in my class. I walked into his office, and he said, "There was no need for you to come in and thank me for the letter."

"That's not why I'm here," I said. "I just wanted to let you know I'm going to take a break from school and go into the army."

This news wasn't exactly what he had anticipated. I needed only about nine more credit hours to graduate; I'd had enough honor points to graduate since the end of my sophomore year. In addition to my grades, I was also treasurer of the business school and captain of the track team. Normally, people like me would get recruited by IBM right out of school, not drop out to go into the army. But that's what I had decided to do.

I went to the enrollment office and enlisted in 1956.

"Sign up for three years and you can go into the Finance Corps at Ft. Benjamin Harrison in Indiana," the sergeant said.

"No, Sir," I said. "I'm in for two years because I have to do it. Not one day more than that."

I didn't want to delay my "real" life any more than that. Although I wasn't sure yet what I wanted to do with my career, I knew it wasn't going to involve the U.S. Army. The one positive thing I foresaw about the army, though, was that I'd get the opportunity to see more of the world—the very thing I'd been dreaming about for years. Maybe it wouldn't be bad, after all.

Chapter Three

ARMY DAYS

The first thing the army taught me was that I had no idea who the average American male was. Until I got there, I thought a high school friend of mine who was a B student at a local university was the average young American male. But when I got into basic training, I came face-to-face with a more accurate picture of what "average" really was—monumentally dumber than I'd pictured. By comparison, my friends were all geniuses.

I was very lucky that a private at the enrollment office had noticed something on my enlistment forms: I'd had two years of ROTC training at Mizzou because it was mandatory there.

"All you have to do is get a letter from your ROTC officer, and you can come in as a PFC with one stripe," he said. A PFC meant private first class, and it was a rank normally given to soldiers who served one year or more in the army. The private who told me about this had been in the army for only four months and wasn't a PFC yet.

If I found the guy today, I'd like to give him $100,000, because he saved my life in the army. That one stripe made all the difference—to the guys in basic training, it meant I was a veteran! Instead of being on kitchen patrol like everyone else, I was charge of quarters. The difference was that kitchen patrol went through 12 hours of pure hell washing dirty, greasy dishes while my main responsibility was just to make sure I awoke early enough each day to wake everyone else up. I got a minor pay raise, too—maybe $25 a month extra—but that wasn't the real perk. The main benefit was that I was a squad leader, so the sergeants treated me like I was one of them instead of a recruit. It was just lucky.

We were at Fort Leonard Wood in the Missouri Ozarks or, as it's been nicknamed due to its desolate and remote location, "Fort Lost in the Woods of Misery." It was the middle of winter, and it was grim. When the sergeant woke us at 4 a.m., he loved to demonstrate his power in sheer vocal volume and irrational punitive measures. One day he said, "Take this door down!" and an underling from the second floor arrived and kicked the door off its hinges. After that, we slept in zero-degree weather with no door. Everything in basic training is about breaking recruits down.

One of the guys in my training group called me "The Professor" and asked me to read to him when his 8-year-old sister sent him a letter from their home in Detroit. It said things like, "Our dog has been sick" and "Mom is OK." He couldn't read it; he was functionally illiterate at 18 years old.

During a shooting exercise, they lined up 10 recruits with M1 rifles, which was a difficult weapon. Maybe one in 10 times your rifle would jam. Behind those 10 recruits were another 10 who were supposed to be smarter recruits, and I was in that group. Our job was to hold onto their ammunition belts and not let them stop, because if the line moved ahead and someone had his weapon cocked sideways, someone could get shot . . . which is exactly what happened to me.

The idiot shot my helmet off my head. It felt like someone had hit me in the head with a sledgehammer. I didn't realize it was a bullet until afterward, when the lieutenant asked whether I was OK and I saw the shrapnel.

"What happened?" I asked.

"The guy next to you stopped and his weapon discharged," he said.

It's one of the military's dark secrets—you just don't hear about the people who die in training exercises, but it happens quite a bit.

Our company consisted of about 380 people, and only two of us got three-day passes during the eight weeks of training. I won the physical training contest because I was still in shape from track season, and the other guy was the best marksman because he was a rich kid who grew up skeet shooting. I took him to St. Louis on our break, and after training, he took me to his hometown, Bloomfield Hills, Michigan.

When basic training ended, most soldiers were shipped out to Korea. My college roommate went to Germany, but I willed myself to France. During college, I had read *Swann's Way* by Marcel Proust, the first volume of *Remembrance of Things Past*, and that's what ignited my love of France. It was required reading, and it took me about a week to read the first 100 pages and about two days to read the next 500. The author describes everything in meticulous detail; I remember being impatient when he took pages to describe drinking chamomile tea and eating madeleine cookies, but once I slowed down and got into the flow, I fell in love with this place he described.

I reveled in my good fortune when I was shipped off on the troops' ship to France—a "deluxe cabin" for 280. I was assigned to the bottom bunk of six, and all five guys above me were seasick, so I went out on the deck. As I stood in the fresh air, looking out on the expanse of rolling blue waves, I was overcome with gratitude. "I'm here! I'm going to France!" I thought. Two boys from Arkansas stood with their arms folded in a sign of complaint. "I've gotta be here for a year and a half," one said to the other. Then a gull pooped right on their heads. That's the difference between a good attitude and a bad attitude.

We arrived in Europe and rode a train all night through Germany and then to France. I couldn't sleep; I just wanted to study every detail of the little German towns through the windows. They looked like the model houses under our Christmas tree back home. It was the best time of my life to that point. For the first time, I had the monkey off my back: I didn't have to make As, I didn't have to run faster and harder, and I was traveling in Europe—my dream come true.

Everything was smaller in Europe—telephone poles, roads. One of my first impressions of France was of the beautiful streets that were tree lined on both sides and free of litter. Things looked old yet clean and proper. Fields seemed more like gardens than farms. I felt like I was in a glamorous place covered in history.

People told me that the French could be snobbish toward Americans, but I never had any trouble. It took me years to figure out why, but it's because I was walking around saying, "I can't believe I'm in France! Oh, what a wonderful country. It's so beautiful." I didn't speak the language, but how could they be mad at me? I was the walking chamber of commerce.

At the army base, my colonel grabbed me because I had the highest IQ on the post. He was collecting IQs; he thought having the brightest people in his unit gave him prestige. We had company headquarters, which I was in, and then four companies of guards—next to latrine orderlies, the dumbest in the army. Dummies with rifles.

I had a great job as the forms and reports control officer for the biggest ammunition depot in Europe. Headquarters wanted reports on how many hand grenades and missiles and other weapons we had in our depot. I was supposed to assign numbers to everything and keep it orderly.

"That's a chickenshit job," the colonel said. "I don't want you to do anything. Everybody's got to come to us to get a number to send a report out? Baloney. I don't want you to do it. Put any numbers you want on the reports. Just find a way to pass the inspections."

Even better, I had three French girls working under me and enough work for only one. So I divided the job into thirds, and they were quite pleased they'd been fortunate enough to have me as a boss.

We found ways to appear as if we were keeping track. I had a couple of perfect files, so when someone would come to inspect and ask, "Can you show us some of your reports?" I could open up the right drawer and show them only those files.

"Wow, that's exactly right," they'd say, and we'd get the highest ratings on all of our inspections. Little did they know that the rest of the file drawers were filled with waste paper—literally, waste paper. If they had ever opened a drawer and pulled out a file, we all would have been in trouble.

But my colonel was happy, my French workers were happy, and I was delighted to spend my days going to the library and reading. One of the officers who had read my records realized I was an Eagle Scout, so he asked me to become the scoutmaster of a Boy Scout troop for the military's kids. We didn't have a civilian facility, so the married people all lived off the post with their families.

Being an army scoutmaster was a funny experience, much removed from my own Scouting days. When I was a Scout, we were a middle-class troop that saved enough money to buy a broken-down truck to go on paper drives and take us to Scout camp. Here, once I realized that Major Wall, the chief transportation officer, was the father of one of my Scouts, everything was different.

"Sir, I'm taking the boys camping," I told him on the phone one day. "Do you think you could give us some equipment?"

He sent two big army trucks carrying tents and all the supplies we could ever need. Mess sergeants had come to cook for the kids. He had also brought soldiers who began putting up the tents.

"Major Wall, stop!" I said. "I want the Scouts to do this."

It was solid-gold camping. Anything we wanted, we got. It was also sort of a joke, and, fortunately, my stint as scoutmaster was short-lived.

I still had plenty of extra time, so the officers asked me to run the three noncommissioned officer (NCO) clubs for extra duty pay. This meant I was the highest-paid corporal on the base and had one of the easiest jobs.

The army had three levels of clubs: the enlisted men's (EM) clubs, the NCO clubs, and the officers' clubs. My friend Dan Devine ran the officers' club, and my other friend Wally Sugar ran the EM club. They were both from Chicago. Dan was Catholic, Wally was Jewish, and I was Protestant, so we dubbed ourselves "the Unholy Three." We were basically accountants, which I was trained to do, but this was my first practical experience.

The clubs were for drinking and socializing. No food was served. All of the sergeants assigned to work in the clubs had VD. They weren't allowed to cook food, but they could serve drinks, so the higher-ups gave them to me to give them something to do.

I was to keep track of the daily consumption reports at the clubs and make sure things were running smoothly and profitably. The job came with another perk, too: the main bartender at my biggest club was the sergeant major of my company, and he controlled all the passes. We had a great working relationship:

I signed all his paychecks and expense accounts, and he signed all my passes. We never had to discuss it. When no one else on base had a pass, I had one, which meant I got to go to Paris every weekend. At the end of my stint in the army, my commanding officer said, "Good luck in civilian life, Ebsworth. I just have one question for you: how did you get all those passes?" He never did figure it out.

Two of the guys running my clubs were a pair of very likeable sergeants, Friedman and Martinez. I lived in the barracks, and they lived off-base; they were always trying to get me to move in with them so they could corrupt me and get something on me. They were just goof-offs, and their stupidity was astounding. One day, a major came to do inspections.

"Where's your safe, Sergeant?" he asked, and Friedman led him to it. "It's open," the major observed.

"Yes, Sir."

"Why is it open?"

"Because I don't remember the combination," Friedman said.

"You keep your money in an open safe?"

"Oh, no, Sir. I keep it under my mattress, and I sleep on it!"

These were the people I worked with. These same two knuckleheads also reported to the colonel in civilian clothes one day when he'd called for them, and he made them leave to change into their uniforms. When it came to the inventory reports, I couldn't convince one of the sergeants that the word "yes" is spelled with one "s." He continued spelling it "yess."

Then there were the fiddles going on in the club, and I probably wouldn't have figured out any of them on my own. People don't realize that most crimes are solved not by police but by whistle-blowers who call in tips and say, "You'd better look at Charlie." That's how it was with the clubs—someone would tip me off that someone else was ripping off the club in some way.

First was a soldier who would come in every morning, take $20 from the till, and buy a case of beer. He'd return with it and sell it in the club at a profit. He'd replace the $20 he'd originally taken so the till was still right, but then he'd keep all the rest of the profit. Another sergeant who worked for me got tired of hearing, "Hey, don't you have any food in here?" so he bought hard-boiled eggs and sold them in the club. A colonel who commanded the whole base regularly ate there, and it was completely illegal.

Then there was the issue of the exchange rate. In the army, the rule was that if you needed to replenish your French bank account, you wrote a check from your American account to your French account. The exchange rate at the time was 350 francs for one American dollar, but the black market rate was 440 francs to a dollar. We were only about 85 miles from Luxembourg, so prior to my time running the clubs, the men would write a $100,000 check to cash, drive to Luxembourg, and make the exchange. Then they'd come back and put 35,000,000 francs into the account and have 9,000,000 left over, which went into their pockets.

The man who ran the clubs before me was a lieutenant, and he allowed it—he probably split the money with them. But I didn't.

The first time I wrote a check from the American account to the French account, the guys just about died.

"But, Sir," they said—I was a corporal and they called me "Sir"—"that's not the way we usually do it."

"That's the way we're doing it now," I said. "This is what it says in the army regulations, and this is how we're doing it."

If there was a silly little administrative law, I didn't feel bad fudging it a little, but I wouldn't get near a criminal law. It was the sergeants' worst day when I cut off their French franc account. Looking back, I doubt we ever would have been caught. The money was really the club's money, not government funds, so the audits weren't very strict. A few years after I left the army, they created a new honor: "top enlisted man," the highest rank possible. The first top enlisted man was someone who ran the Wagon Wheel club in Frankfurt. The fact that he was first must have buttressed the humiliation for all concerned when he was caught pocketing more than a million dollars a year running a fiddle in that club.

Although I had never been a sheep, the army taught me to be even less of a follower. I've always had the innate ability to figure out the way you're supposed to go, even when everyone else is going the wrong way. It's just a matter of paying attention. And to me, there was no better place to pay attention than Paris.

Chapter Four

FALLING FOR FRANCE

The first time you find something wonderful is the best, and Paris lived up to every one of my fantasies about it. I went there for the first time on a three-day weekend with Wally Sugar and a German American friend whose parents got out of Germany and moved to Rio de Janeiro prior to Hitler's atrocities. For three days, my friend cried all the way through Paris because he said it reminded him of Rio. "I have to go to Rio someday if it's like this," I noted.

We arrived at the Gare de l'Est train station late in the evening and found a cheap place to stay near the station. It turned out to be a rent-by-the-hour third-class hotel. The next morning, we moved on to another hotel about a block off the Champs-Élysées, and it turned out to be the same type of hotel, but at least we were in a better area for touring. I rode the Metro 38 times and learned my way around the city by using maps. Back then, you didn't have to worry about muggings, violent crime, or much of anything, except the occasional pervert.

We went everywhere in those three days: the Arc de Triomphe, the Eiffel Tower, the Sacré-Coeur Basilica, the Pantheon, La Madeleine church, Luxembourg Gardens, Palais-Royale, the Tuileries Gardens. It was amazing.

One of those first stops turned out to be a life changer for me: the Louvre museum.

Built in 1190 as a fortress, then redesigned as a royal palace, the Louvre became a museum in 1793. Of course, I knew that it was one of the largest and most visited art museums in the world, but I was not an art connoisseur. I visited it because it was such an integral part of Paris, and what I found there changed me.

At that time (before I. M. Pei's glass pyramid), the inconsequential side-door entrance barely hinted at what was inside: on the left a grand staircase and the Winged Victory of Samothrace marble statue from the early second century B.C. I couldn't help but revere the majesty of the statue. It was completely different from seeing pictures in art books. Seeing it in person was an *experience*.

Although I'd been to a few art museums before, this was certainly the most impressive. I walked from exhibit to exhibit in awe of how it felt to be surrounded by such great works of art. Leaving was difficult, but when I did, I found that the Louvre had ignited a new curiosity in me. I wanted to know more about the works I had seen—I wanted to understand the pictures, the time periods they were from, the artists who had created them.

Before long, I was spending considerable hours in the library during the week researching for my next trips to the Louvre. With no mentor and no formal classes, I trained myself in art history just by reading and looking. My eyes were my mentors.

I was more drawn to Western work than Eastern, but any work of great quality interested me. In the beginning, it irritated me that artists were so reluctant to talk about their work, but over time, I learned to respect that. One artist explained it something like this: "If I wanted to explain my art, I would have become a writer, not a painter. I just paint. It's up to you to figure out what it means."

My own artistic abilities were completely absent. I never showed any promise in art—but that's OK. You have to know your own strengths. My aptitude to learn about other people's art far exceeded my ability to create art.

New Year's Eve of 1956 going into 1957 was coming up, and I wanted to do something. I'm a nostalgic person, and to me, instead of the beginning of a new year, New Year's Eve represented the end of an old year. It was always sort of a melancholy occasion, and "Auld Lang Syne" just made me feel sadder. That year, I suggested that "the Unholy Three" ask for a three-day pass so we could go to Paris and at least spend the holiday together.

Before living in France, I really didn't drink alcohol. It wasn't for religious reasons so much as it was for training reasons—I had been trying to qualify for the Olympic team and kept my body as pure as I could. Wine was such a major part of the culture in France, though, that I'd had at least had a few drinks here and there since I'd been in the army. But on this particular occasion, I got drunk for the first time. The night before New Year's Eve, we drank a lot of champagne, and I was very hung over the next day.

At 6:00 on New Year's Eve, we were all supposed to go out for dinner on the town, but I said, "Guys, go have fun. I feel terribly sick. There's no point in my ruining your evening. I'm just going to stay in."

They left, and I slept. Four hours later, I awoke feeling much better . . . and hungry. I wandered out of the hotel in search of something to eat. I was all alone in the city and had no idea where the guys had gone. I didn't speak French, and by then it was just over an hour until midnight.

"What am I doing here?" I thought. I didn't want to spend New Year's Eve alone, so when I saw the USO, it was a welcome sight. I always wore civilian clothes off-base, and I didn't want any part of identifying as a GI, but at least this was a place where I could say "Happy New Year" in English.

Inside, people were dancing and celebrating together—some troops and some locals. At about 10 minutes before midnight, I noticed a cute French girl dancing with a soldier. I assumed she must have been his steady, which disappointed me. But five minutes later, he left her. Maybe the pressure of knowing that you're supposed to kiss the person you're with at midnight got to him.

Never one to be slow on the uptake, I moved in and introduced myself and started dancing with her right at the stroke of midnight. Her name was Martine, she was 19 years old, and little did I know that she was going to be my wife.

The USO was a Goody Two-shoes type of place that closed at 12:30, and I was not ready to let Martine go, so I asked her to go out with me.

"There's this new place around the corner called Whisky à Go Go," I said. "We can go there and dance."

"Well," she said with some hesitation. "I'm here with my older sister . . ."

Martine and her older sister, Christiane, were both studying English and had come to the USO to practice. Martine introduced me for Christiane's approval. I must have passed inspection, because she gave permission for us to stay out that night.

We went to the Whisky and danced until after the Metro stopped running at 2 a.m. It wouldn't start again until 6 a.m., so now we had no choice—we *had* to stay! At 6:00, she said to me, "The Metro is running again. I have to get home."

"I'll take you home," I said.

She resisted—my hotel was in the opposite direction, and she didn't want to inconvenience me.

"You don't understand. Americans always take their dates home at the end of the night. I insist," I said—which was partly to be chivalrous but more because I really wanted to find out where she lived so I wouldn't lose her.

When we got back to her apartment, I said, "I want my buddies to meet you."

"I'll be back at the USO at 4 p.m.," she said.

We'd just make it. Wally and Dan and I had to take a train back to base at 6:00, so we'd have a little while to see Martine again before we had to leave.

I took the Metro back to the hotel, and it was 8 a.m. by the time I got to the room. Wally Sugar rolled over, opened one eye, and said, "Sick, huh?"

I told them about this wonderful girl I'd met, and they headed to the USO with me that afternoon to see for themselves . . . but she never showed. The whole ride back on the train, the guys ribbed me. "Suuuure, you met this girl," they said.

I was disappointed until I got a letter about a week later that said, "I'm sorry I couldn't get back in time. We were having a family celebration, and I was waiting on the oysters."

She had gone back to the USO at 6:00, right after we'd left, and she wanted to see me again.

From then on, I spent every weekend in Paris with Martine. For a while, I took trains and secured rides with people, but eventually, I wanted my own transportation. My sergeant tried to talk me into buying his five-year-old Mercedes, but I bought a new Volkswagen for the same price instead because I wanted a more economical car for when I returned for law school.

We visited the Louvre every Saturday. I'm sure that Martine wouldn't have spent so much time in the museum had it not been for me, but she also appreciated art. I studied the work until I could easily have been one of the tour guides; I could give you a room-by-room description of every picture.

After the Louvre, we'd have lunch and walk in the Tuileries or Luxembourg Gardens. Before long, her parents invited me to stay with them on the weekends.

Martine and I were in love. It was such a happy time that I turned down what would have been a dream job for me in other circumstances: the army invited me to coach its European track team. I was just a year out of running competitively by that point and would have loved to get back into it, but it would have meant giving up my weekends in Paris with Martine. What I had was so good that I didn't want to chance losing it. It was like being on vacation every weekend.

In March 1957, I was heading to Italy for 10 days. I had booked the trip before I met Martine, and now I didn't want to leave her. I had no choice, though, because she was still in school. The trip was through a German travel agency that specialized in tours for GIs, and it consisted of 10 days in Capri, Naples, Rome, Pisa, Florence, and Venice. We stayed in nice hotels and ate three meals a day. The tour cost $99. I had no idea how the company made any money. A year later it went bankrupt.

While I was gone, I thought about Martine so much that I proposed as soon as I got back, even though we'd known each other for only three months. I gave her my Kansas relay medal, and she said yes. After that, all the trips I took I took with her. In the year and a half I was in Europe, we went to London, Glasgow, Edinburgh, Florence, Rome, Venice, Munich, and all through Switzerland. Everywhere we went we visited art museums.

Martine and I were going to get married that July, but two things made me change my mind. First was the thought that I was on active duty and could get reassigned at any time, leaving a new wife behind, and second was the part of my brain that wanted to slow down, go home, and make sure that this was real and not just a French romance.

She understood, and we agreed that she'd stay in school in France and I'd go back to the States and we'd take a little more time to make sure we knew what we were doing. My sister had come to France to be the maid of honor, but when I changed the plan at the last minute, the three of us went to Great Britain for three weeks instead of having a wedding. It rained hard every day, but the trip was wonderful. We got to meet our grandmother and aunt for the first time. It would be the only time we would see my grandmother. I spent a weekend with my Aunt Muriel a few years later.

After my two years in the army were over, I went home to St. Louis for law school . . . for two hours.

Why am I doing this? I thought. My mind wasn't on law studies; it was busy thinking about how to get back to France so I could marry Martine. She and I kept in touch frequently by letters; international phone calls were too expensive then.

I had been offered a job in France with the U.S. Department of the Army, but I didn't like the idea of the government having control of my life. I wanted to find my way back to Europe on my own terms. Although I never intended to live in Europe permanently, I loved being there and wanted to travel through more of it.

I also realized that my feelings for Martine were real, as were hers for me. We set a new date, and I sailed back to France, where we married in March of 1958. No one from my family could attend. Muriel was teaching school and couldn't take off. My army buddy Gene Czerwinsky was my best man. We had a great French reception. My friend Bob Ahern loaned me his black Volkswagen as a wedding present.

We painted two hearts on the back of the car with an arrow through them, and inside the hearts we wrote "USA" and "F" for France, with the words "Just Married" in French and English on top. As we drove off on our two-week honeymoon on the Riviera, people honked and waved. Martine's aunt had given us $125 in francs as a wedding present, which was enough to cover a week's stay, including all meals, at the L'Oasis hotel in La Napoule. The room was tiny and damp, but the food was terrific.

Fifteen years later, the owner was the visiting guest chef at the Oriental Hotel in Bangkok, where I happened to be staying.

I said, "I stayed with you in March of 1958. Full pension for two for one week was $125." By this time, the hotel was closed, but the restaurant had three Michelin stars.

"Oh . . ." he said. "I don't think I remember you."

At the end of our honeymoon, I took the Volkswagen to be washed before taking it back to Bob. But there was one little problem: the sun had baked our message into the paint.

"If this doesn't come off, have it painted and I'll pay for it," I told him. I don't know whether it ever did come off, but he never asked me for any money.

After our honeymoon, I brought Martine back to the United States. We moved into a $65-per-month apartment in South St. Louis, and I decided to let IBM hire me.

"We don't hire in April," they said. Plus, they wanted to hire people right from graduation, not two years after school.

Fine, I thought. *I'll go to NCR instead.*

But NCR didn't want to hire me, either, so I put a sales campaign on both of them, showing them why they should hire me. Then they both offered me jobs, and I took great pleasure in turning them down.

For the next year, I worked in insurance, and Martine worked as a secretary. I analyzed insurance policies for a million-dollar roundtable fellow who was selling big policies. The job was decent paying, but there were more Mondays than there were Saturdays.

"I can do well at anything I want to do," I said to myself. "So what do I really want to do?"

Since travel was such a passion of mine, I decided that working for a travel company would suit me. After much campaigning, I finally found work with Kirkland Deluxe Travel in St. Louis as a sales agent—and that's where my career began.

Chapter Five

THE TRAVEL BUSINESS

Velma Jane Livergood was the fifth woman to marry Joe Kirkland, and she became Jane Kirkland overnight.

"How can anyone be married five times?" I thought. Then again, Artie Shaw had done it eight times.

Joe had four offices around St. Louis: Clayton, downtown, Belleville, and South St. Louis. Jane became the manager of the Clayton office.

Just a month after I was hired, Joe died, and Jane became my boss.

"You can't type," she said one day, watching me at the typewriter. "How did you type your application letter?"

"I typed it," I said. "You didn't ask how long it took me to type it."

She didn't like me, but she had to keep me on because she was so insecure and had no idea how to run a business. I was a man, and I had a car, so she shipped me off to South St. Louis—at least for a while. In the year I worked for her, I moved back and forth 10 times, running every office. She was having problems with the Belleville office, so she closed it and then closed the other two offices, too, leaving only the Clayton location. All she did was milk the company. She paid herself her own salary, plus her late husband's salary.

One day, she'd said something to irritate me, and I said, "You've got to be the highest-paid secretary in the world."

We were getting to the end of our time together by then.

Meanwhile, a travel company across the river in Alton, Illinois, had started a branch office next to St. Louis University. The company was called International Travel Advisors, and its owner, Sully Sullivan, was a wonderful guy but a terrible businessman who was running out of money. He brought in a partner, John Jenkins, who owned a surgical supply and medical bookstore. Jenkins bought half the business for $5,000 in 1959, and the manager quit shortly thereafter.

They needed a new manager, so Sully talked to some airline sales managers who said, "Barney Ebsworth's been in the business for only a year, but he's sharp. He's going somewhere."

They hired me, and I went to work in this dingy little office that used to be a wig shop in a rundown part of town. The rumor was that a bookie joint was operating upstairs. The only employee was Jenkins's daughter, and the first thing I did was fire her. Nice girl but she couldn't do the job.

"I might as well find out how much power I have in this job," I thought. No one gave me a hard time about it, which I took as a good sign. I hired a lady I knew.

Being a travel agent was up my alley. I was very good at sales and marketing—delivering the right pitches to the right people and knowing how to treat clients. We turned a profit within that first year. Before the year was up, I'd been offered a job as the district sales manager for the Dutch airline KLM for a lot more money, but I really wanted to stay in the travel agency business.

I went to Jenkins and said, "I really want to stay here, but I want to be a partner."

Unbeknownst to me, Sully was running out of money again—which was an ongoing problem. So when Jenkins talked to him about my proposal, Sully offered to let me buy him out.

"You can buy half the company for $5,000," Jenkins told me.

"I don't have $5,000," I said—but Jenkins was ready to take care of that. He went to the bank and cosigned on a loan for the full amount. Now I was half owner of International Travel Advisors.

Our business was mostly selling airline tickets. We'd make 5 percent selling a domestic ticket, 7 percent selling an international ticket, and 10 percent selling tours. That's how we kept the lights on, just waiting for people to walk into the office or call up because they'd seen our ads in the newspaper. Sometimes people would book their hotels or resorts through us, but our main income was from airline tickets. I realized early on that we needed to find ways to make better margins and to drum up more business, and a good way to do both was by packaging our own tours.

When you package your own tours, you buy the elements of the package and sell them together. We could get group rates on airlines, hotels, and attractions. Not only do you lower the cost for customers and make better profits but also you're manufacturing business rather than waiting for customers to walk through the door—you're out there soliciting them and giving them ideas about trips they might like to take. During the day, I made sales calls, and I did office work at night. Every night, I worked until at least 8:00, sometimes 9:00 or 10:00, but I always took Sundays off.

The tours were all designed for special-interest groups. I can't take credit for the first one I did because it wasn't my idea. I ate a lot of my meals at a big cafeteria down the block from the agency, and Harry Pope, the barrel-chested guy who owned the cafeteria, also owned two others. He had 600 employees, and he also ran an organization called the Food Service Management Guild. Lots of well-to-do restaurant owners from around the world belonged to the guild. Harry had been buying airline tickets at the agency, but now he had a bigger idea.

"I'm thinking about doing a tour of Europe for my members in the United States. Will you set up the arrangements for me?" he asked.

At the time, I'd been with International Travel Advisors for only about six months, and the opportunity was exciting. There wasn't much creativity involved on my part; I mostly took notes like an assistant while Harry told me where he wanted his members to go:

Copenhagen, Stockholm, Milan, Zurich, Paris, and London. They would tour the best restaurants in all of those cities to get ideas. I made the reservations and set them up with a tour agent. Harry had a bigger operation than any of the food services they visited, and they rolled out the red carpet for him. I didn't make a big commission because they were really his contacts, but that didn't matter; he started me in the tour business.

His trip lit the fuse for me. It got my mind working by thinking about what other special-interest groups might be interested in personalized tours and how to pitch to them. Each group needed some kind of hook.

At Washington University, I went to the head of the alumni association and said, "You're always trying to raise money—what if I put together an alumni tour of Europe for you? You have a postgraduate center here; give me a professor of European history and we'll feature him as a tour guide. You don't have to worry about anything. I'll create the brochure and send out the mailings and put the whole trip together."

They agreed to it, as did many others. We did 21-day tours in which we'd spend brief amounts of time at some of the major highlights of Europe. I called them "rat races" because of the hectic pace. We'd fly to London, cross over to Holland by boat, and get on a bus. When I think about it now, it reminds me very much of the Mel Stuart movie *If It's Tuesday, This Must Be Belgium*.

The benefit to the school or organization was a commission and some free tickets. For every 15 people who booked, I was able to give a free trip, but I liked to sell it as two free tickets for every

30 booked. That way I could say, "If we get 30 people, you and your wife [or husband] can come for free."

Success came quickly. I created tours for churches, schools, golf organizations, and other groups, but it was a lot of work. I had to come up with the ideas, make all the arrangements, do all the marketing, track the reservations, coordinate with the vendors, and keep everyone happy. We had three employees by then who wrote the tickets and did assorted office tasks, but I was the sole salesperson and marketer.

Working with Jenkins was becoming more and more problematic for me. We just had entirely different philosophies about how to run a business. If, for example, the going rate for a book-keeper was $400 a month, I'd rather pay $500 and get the best bookkeeper. Jenkins, however, would rather pay $300 for someone barely qualified. "Why would you inflict that on yourself to save $100 a month?" I thought.

And every year, he'd take a free trip worth about $5,000. Finally, around 1962, I knew it was time to change this relationship. "John, we've come to a parting of the ways," I said. "There are three things we can do, and since it's my suggestion, I'll let you choose. You can buy me out, I can buy you out, or I can walk out. Which one do you want?"

He said that since the company's net worth was about $32,000, he'd give me $16,000 for my half.

"What do you want for your half?" I asked.

"$50,000."

"My half is worth $16,000, and your half is worth $50,000?"

"Yes."

"I have an alternate offer. I'll pay you $5,000 now and $5,000 a year for the next nine years."

I knew I could afford to pay the $5,000 up front, and he was going to take a $5,000 trip every year anyway, so it was like 10 years of free trips. He took the deal.

He made me put all the stock in escrow with the bank until I paid him off. Business improved after he left, and I made $150,000 the following year. Even though paying him off early would cost more, I just couldn't wait to say "adios." So I paid him his $40,000, and our association ended. The business was officially mine, and I've been happy ever since.

The 1960s saw the rise of commercial jet aircrafts as the way to travel internationally, and it changed the travel industry. Now, instead of spending six days at sea to get to Europe, you could get there in six hours. Given the choice, most people said, "I'll take six hours, please!"

It was a great time to be in the industry. Many people who couldn't have taken the time to travel by ship were now able to see places they never imagined they'd see in their lifetimes. My clientele were not all wealthy people; some were, to be sure, but we also had a lot of students and teachers. Even though the fares were a lot of money for many people, it was worth it to them to find out what else was out there in this big world.

I had promised my childhood friend Larry Douglass that I would take a trip with him anywhere in the world when he graduated from medical school in the early 1960s.

"I want to go to Zermatt and climb the Matterhorn," he said.

Well, I had said anywhere, and he had humored me when we took our Pikes Peak trip, so I agreed. Before our trip, I went to Zermatt with Martine and her family to survey the situation. I threw open the drapes in our hotel room at 8:00 in the morning and caught my first glimpse of this white dagger of a mountain.

"What have I gotten myself into?" I thought. I had been told that it was a hike, but it really wasn't—it was just a climb straight up in the air. Balance isn't one of my strong points.

We walked through the town toward the mountain and came upon the largest cemetery I've ever seen in a small town—and the average age of the deceased was about 22. It's a burial ground for people of all nationalities who've lost their lives on the Matterhorn.

"I think you're crazy, but I'll do it with you," I told Larry.

On the week of the hundredth anniversary of the first climb, I stood there with my new climbing equipment and fancy climbing shoes and approached the Riffelhorn, a preliminary climb to the Matterhorn.

Seth Graben, our Swiss guide, started the climb ahead of us, straight up a 55-foot boulder.

"Come on," he called after us.

"Come on where?" I asked.

"Come on here!"

"But . . . how?"

It was like trying to figure out how to scale the face of a three-story house. Seth pulled my rope tight, and I started climbing.

Somehow I managed to get to the top, which had a beautiful view of the Matterhorn.

"Have you ever had anybody on this mountain as scared as me?"

He pondered for a few seconds and said, "Yes, last year I had an American girl who was worse than you."

It seemed to be a double shot at me (American *and* a girl), but I didn't feel too bad about it because I was too preoccupied with being terrified. The next day we hiked to the start of the Matterhorn climb. We slept that night in a hut with about 80 people who were coughing and snoring and tossing and turning. At 3 a.m., our guides awoke us to start the day because by about 8:00, the clouds at the top begin forming. From below, the clouds are beautiful, but near the top, it's a perpetual snowstorm. Because of this, it's best to be at the top of the Matterhorn by 8:00 so you can be on your way down when the weather turns bad.

So in the pitch black, we walked 20 or 30 yards until Seth said, "OK, let's go."

I couldn't see anything, but I reached my hand out and felt ice-cold rock. That's what I would be climbing all the way up the mountain. Everyone had individual guides up the Matterhorn—I stuck with Seth, and Larry was assigned to Seth's brother, Herbert, who had just carried the BBC's TV cameras up the mountain the week before to film a documentary about the hundredth anniversary of the first climb.

Our two teams lost each other quickly. About halfway up, Seth asked me to hold on for a minute. It turned out that two German boys had been stuck overnight on the mountain because their ropes were too short to properly make the climb. They'd made it to a little resting hut and were waiting for help. They climbed over Seth's back, down our rope, and over my back to start their way down the mountain.

After that stunt, I stopped to take a rest at the last small hut on the mountain, where I came upon a white-haired woman who appeared to be about 70 years old emerging in her climbing gear, looking like this was no big deal to her. I felt silly for struggling.

When we were about 600 feet from the top of the mountain, Seth climbed like a cat about 80 feet above me on a straight vertical path and then called after me to follow him.

The thought still makes me sweat today, 57 years later. Where could I possibly get a foothold? I wore steel crampons to help me dig into the ice and snow, but this was nearly bare rock. I dug my fingers into any crack I could find, but even so, I lost my grip about halfway up. I began sliding down, quickly gaining momentum, and my only thought was that I had to catch the ledge below. My speed was so great, however, that I bounced right over the ledge and fell to the end of the rope. I was 7,000 feet above the Theodul Glacier. It was so far below me that it looked like a map.

I have no real recollection of how I got out of this situation, except that I guess I climbed hand-over-hand up the rope in terror. That was good enough for me. Larry made it to the top, and I didn't see him again until we were both back at our hotel room in town.

In 1961, I took my first around-the-world trip, and I visited India for the first time. The poverty was difficult to experience. I even saw dead bodies lying in the street.

Our next stop was Cairo. The Nile Hilton had been open only a year, and when we arrived, I was so relieved that I thought, "I'm home!" Other people from the United States who had just come straight to Cairo didn't feel that way, but I was so thankful to be anywhere other than India.

On my second night in the hotel, I was meeting someone in the lobby for dinner at 8:00, so I headed out to the elevator a bit early—being punctual was important to me. I stood outside the closed elevator doors and pressed the "down" button. After a minute or two, I noticed the sound of the elevator whooshing by.

"Hmm," I thought. "Wonder why it didn't stop."

Then another one whooshed by and then another. I was on the twelfth floor and didn't fancy the idea of taking the stairs all the way down to my meeting and arriving sweaty and out of breath, so I waited and waited, picturing my friend getting perturbed down in the lobby. Finally, at 8:30, the doors opened, and the elevator was already packed. There was no way I was letting this one get by, though, so I pushed my way in, ending up pressed right up against a rather large man. The doors closed, and I looked down and realized I was belly to belly with the president of Yugoslavia, Marshal Tito.

His two bodyguards were on either side of him, and without saying anything, one of them turned me around and pushed me against the door. I found out later that Tito was there to meet with

Colonel Gamal Abdel Nasser, the prime minister of Egypt. Some kind of reception was taking place on the top floor, which is why they had blocked off all the elevators.

My friend in the lobby was able to forgive my tardiness when I explained that I had just been intimate with Marshal Tito.

It was my first up-close encounter with a famous person, but it would be far from my last. My work and my hobbies would both lead me to meet celebrities from the worlds of art, entertainment, and politics—but that wasn't even on my radar then. What was on my radar was trying to find a level of economic stability that would allow me to feel safe.

No longer was I worried about making $12,000 a year; now I was thinking bigger.

"If I had $250,000 in the bank earning 5 percent, no matter what happened to me, that money would always provide for my family," I thought. I always hoped to have a family. So that became my new goal. I went back to work with a renewed desire to find this kind of comfort.

After I executed a few successful tours with Washington University, the school invited me to open a branch office on campus. It was a great opportunity and fit into my plans to expand the company. We served the teaching and administrative staff as well as students and alumni.

Only one other person in town was doing creative travel, and that was Fritz Weedhouse. He did choir tours, and I admired him. He would have been formidable competition for me, so I was glad we weren't really competing—his choir tour business was all over the country, not focused on St. Louis. Aside from him, I had carved out my own niche.

For my first seven years in the travel business, I generally slept every other night. It's not that I was working around the clock but that I felt so much pressure that I just couldn't sleep. There was no way to rest on your laurels when you always had to ensure that the next tour would fill and that things would run smoothly. I don't remember ever having to cancel a tour because it didn't meet the minimum numbers, but the problem for me was that there was a significant profit difference between the minimum and the maximum. I didn't want to make $5,000 on a tour with 20 people when I could make $25,000 on a tour with 35 people.

It's amazing the way I tolerated stress. Despite the sleep deprivation, I stayed healthy and never missed a day of work.

I tried to find ways to unwind and spend time with Martine. In the late summer every year, we sailed to Europe. The ships were ocean liners, which differ significantly from modern cruise ships.

Ocean liners then were really just a means of travel from point A to point B, like floating hotels. There may have been some entertainment, such as a singer or small band, but nothing significant. Same with gyms—some of the larger ships may have had small gyms, but they were nothing like the facilities people expect now. The ships had three classes: first class, cabin class, and tourist class. The first-class rooms included showers and bathtubs, but tourist class had only common showers and toilets. Sometimes the bottom cabins didn't even have any windows. Passengers from the bottom two classes were always trying to sneak over to see what the first-class cabins looked like, whereas the rich kids in first class were trying to sneak past their parents and nannies to get into tourist class, where most of the kids were.

I sailed on Cunard's *Queen Mary* and *Queen Elizabeth*, Holland America's *Rotterdam*, United States Line's *United States*, the French Line's *Liberté*, and the maiden voyage of the Italian Line's *Michelangelo*.

Each summer, Martine and I would fly to New York, catch a Broadway show, spend the night in the city, and then sail the following day and spend five to seven days at sea. I loved being at sea with nothing much to do—it gave me a pause between my hectic work life and touring Europe. I didn't know that I was experiencing the end of the passenger era and that jets would soon "sink" the ocean liner business.

Martine would stay with her family in Paris for a month after I came home, which probably didn't have the best effect on our marriage. We were trying to have a baby, something we both deeply desired. My wish was to have three daughters. I was afraid to have sons because I figured I'd push them just as hard as my dad pushed me.

At work, I expanded the network of organizations we served. We picked up some golf groups, more schools, and other athletic associations. I would often fly out to Europe to join a tour for a couple of days and then fly to the next one for a couple of days. The reasons were threefold: it gave me another excuse to be in Europe, I could check out how things were going on the tours, and it gave me the opportunity to rub elbows with the key people in the organizations who'd be in charge of booking another tour with us the next year.

On one of our European tours with the Mary Institute, tour guide Collette Ely ran into some trouble trying to get the bus gassed. After the tank was full and she went to pay, the attendant said, "We don't take vouchers. You have to pay in cash."

She said, "You will take these vouchers, or you will *suck it out*." They took the vouchers.

I relied on the tour guides to do most of the communicating with the locals. Even after spending so much time in Europe and marrying a French woman, I didn't speak any language other than English. Language is just not one of my talents—I can usually figure out what people are saying in French, but I can't speak it myself. I rationalized that this was a benefit in my line of business, however; I had to hire people who would work with Americans, so wasn't it smart to find out which agents spoke the best English?

The area of my brain that should have been used for language skills was instead dominated by business sense. I was trying to figure out how to build a Rolls-Royce on a Ford assembly line. I kept searching for a breakthrough—a way to increase the profits per trip.

I knew that if I chartered an entire plane, I'd make a much bigger profit—if I could fill it, of course. At least I didn't have to come up with any up-front money. No one ever asked me for deposits in those days. I could promote a tour without ever making any down payments to the airlines, hotels, or vendors, even when I was new to the industry. And that was lucky.

I went back to Washington University and asked, "Would you consider doing a charter from St. Louis to London?" The school said yes. It was the first charter plane to fly from St. Louis to Europe.

By 1965, I was earning a significant income but still working 80 hours per week. A fellow who was in the record business until he suffered a heart attack contacted me to talk about a business proposition for one of his sons. Both sons were attending Harvard, and one had indicated an interest in the charter travel business.

"My son is going to graduate next year, and I'd love for him to come back home," he said. "I thought if I bought your company . . ."

He had money from selling his record distribution company and wanted to buy International Travel Advisors. We agreed on $350,000 and had a contract drawn. We set a date to meet for lunch to sign the contract.

One day before that date, I got a call from the chancellor of Washington University.

"Can I have lunch with you tomorrow?" he asked.

This was my biggest customer, and under normal circumstances, I would have had lunch with him at 3:00 in the morning in Forest Park if he wanted to, but this time, I couldn't.

"I'm sorry," I said. "I have a lunch meeting tomorrow with someone, and I don't know how to contact him before then because he's traveling. I can meet you before or after, though."

"Fine," he said. "Be here at 3 p.m. tomorrow."

At my lunch meeting, I looked at that contract and knew I wasn't ready to make it official. I told the man, "Look, I'm about to leave for Europe for two weeks. Let me think about it, and I'll give you my answer when I come back."

He went ahead and signed the contract . . . now it was just waiting for my signature. I went on to meet the chancellor, who said, "This may come as a surprise to you, but I want you to come work for the university. I'd like you to be the vice chancellor handling external affairs for the university. You'd be in charge of all the moneymaking activities of the university—the bookstore, cafeterias, travel company, everything."

He was right; it was a surprise! I started laughing, and he asked, "What's so funny?"

"There are two things you don't know: one is that I own the company."

"Oh, you're right. I knew you were the manager; I didn't know you owned it."

"Yes, it's my business," I said. "And the other thing is—remember my lunch appointment that I couldn't cancel? I have a signed contract in my pocket to sell my travel company."

One hour after I got a contract to buy my company, I got a job offer. Life's funny.

"Well, then, we can do something," he said. Then he started really pitching me the job.

I said, "Vice chancellors are usually PhDs. You realize that I don't have a degree from the university."

"Yes, I knew that."

"I'm very flattered. I will seriously consider it, but I'm going to Europe for two weeks. Then I'll give you an answer."

I did—and turned both down. Thank goodness. If I had sold the business then, I probably would have reinvented myself, but it wouldn't have been as much fun.

Looking back, I don't think I was ever serious about selling the company then. I had other offers through the years, but I think I was just assessing my own resolve at that point. There were many more avenues to try and aspects of the business I hadn't solved yet that still excited me.

In 1966, I ran our first tours to Asia, and they were very successful. I was on the cusp of making a big breakthrough, but something was still holding me back. I was still steeped in the comfort of St. Louis, rarely moving beyond the city to target any other groups for specialized travel. I just didn't have enough time to travel around making contacts in other areas. I decided that something needed to change if we were going to get bigger.

Two concepts came up. The first was "Travel Calling," which would be run like "Avon Calling." I still wish I had given that a try!

The second was to build another Barney Ebsworth. At first, I thought I could find and mentor someone promising and turn him into a second me—a workaholic who'd be able to do as much as I was doing. Then I realized that was a silly idea, because if I ever did find another Barney Ebsworth, he'd be smart enough to leave me as soon as he'd learned the business enough to strike out on his own. Then I'd have just created my own competition.

Instead, though, maybe I could hire specialists to do parts of my job. For starters, I could hire other salespeople to help, teaching them just one aspect of my job—that way they'd know enough to be really useful but not enough to start their own companies. The first salesman I took on was formerly an Adler typewriter salesman. I didn't want to hire someone who had been selling IBM, because it's too easy to walk in and sell something when everyone already knows your brand. I wanted the guy who had experience selling an unknown—a small company competing with the big guns who could get his foot in the door. Essentially, that's what he was going to have to do for me: approach organizations and sell them on something entirely new, convincing them of our good reputation and reliability despite the fact that we were just a small company with about eight employees.

By the end of that year, I made a decision. 1967 was going to be the big one. We were going to expand all over the country, and my little travel company was going to shoot for the stars. I dubbed it my "B or B" year: big time or bankruptcy.

Chapter Six

INTRAV

It really started with one of the top surgeons from Ohio. He was the group leader on one of our "rat race" tours that I had joined. We drove all day from Geneva to Paris, and when we got there, I said, "Come on, Ed, I'll take you out."

We went to the Follies and then hit a couple of bars. We didn't get in until 4:00 in the morning, both half in the bag.

"This is the first time I've been drunk since medical school," he said.

We had a wonderful time. Then he told me he had to be up by 8:00 in the morning for a sightseeing trip.

All through the following day, it just bothered me. "What in the world?" I thought. "This guy makes $500,000 a year, and he's on vacation. He got up at 8 a.m. for a $6 sightseeing tour. He should have slept until noon and had a private car take him on a personalized sightseeing tour."

I ruminated about why people would do something like that and came to the conclusion that they thought they had to because it was part of the package they bought. "This is included in my tour. I'm burning the money I spent on this trip!" they were thinking, when really, all they were wasting was a $6 sightseeing tour. They could just take it the next day or skip it and spend the morning doing whatever they really wanted to do, like sleeping.

So I came up with a new concept that made more sense. First, I decided to take out the sightseeing and make it optional. In doing so, I was able to bring down the price by about $150. I thought, "Everyone needs a plane ticket and a ride from the airport to the hotel. Everyone will get a first-class hotel to stay in and an American breakfast the next morning. I'll find 10 great restaurants to choose from for dinner and set up a hospitality desk at the hotel to arrange sightseeing and whatever else they want . . . and I'll do it all for $898."

The risk came from my next move. I decided to charter 10 planes to do back-to-back charters. I also more than doubled our staff, which now consisted of about 20 people.

To go with my new concept, I thought it was time to give the business a new, catchier name. From now on, we would be known as INTRAV.

Over the course of several months, I worked out the details. First I needed to figure out where we were going. I wanted someplace exotic that would offer the greatest dollar value and be comfortable and secure, and the place that fit was the Orient.

Travelers would spend four nights in deluxe hotels in Tokyo, Kyoto, and Hong Kong.

I contracted with Northwest Orient Airlines for 10 Boeing 707s with first-class meals and an open bar throughout the flights. The idea of back-to-back charters is like playing baseball and getting all bases loaded. The first group flies into Tokyo (first base). Four days later, the second group flies to Tokyo, and the first moves on to Kyoto (second base) by bullet train. Four days later, the third group flies to Tokyo, the second group goes to Kyoto, and the first group goes to Hong Kong (third base). When the fourth group flies to Tokyo, everyone shifts again, and the first group flies home—and so on. From there on, the airplane and block of hotel rooms are 100 percent filled, and the profits are great. If I could fill the charters with 165 passengers at a time, it would be "big time." On the other hand, if I couldn't, I was going to fail badly.

Charter landing rights were a major hurdle in the equation. Japan had a long and tedious procedure to get approvals. No one had ever done back-to-back charters before, but we were successful in the negotiations.

After securing the hotels and restaurants and the local tour operators, all that was left was getting the passengers, which was the biggest challenge.

My targets were the larger athletic and social clubs. I needed to convince these clubs to buy into the idea of promoting a special trip for their members.

I already had a contact at the Missouri Athletic Club, so that's where we started first, and then we went to the Indianapolis Athletic Club and the Illinois Athletic Club.

Next we found two clubs in Texas that wanted the program: the Cipango Club and the Cork Club. At the time, Texas was a dry state, and the only way you could have a cocktail was in a private club. So, essentially, these exclusive social clubs were set up so people could drink. You had to pay steep membership fees and prove a certain net worth to join the clubs, and they'd attract famous talent to perform for their membership.

I developed a direct mail promotion including a full-color brochure, a cover letter, and an envelope all imprinted with the name of the sponsoring organization. This told the members that the organization approved the travel and vouched for the quality of our offer.

"Now two can travel for the price of one!" the brochures said. The bargain really was astounding—not only were they traveling by chartered jet direct from their hometowns but also everything was first class, from the hotels to the food, and they'd have unlimited menu choices at the finest restaurants. Our dining slogan was "The choice is yours; the check is ours."

While I paced around my office, the mailings hit their targets. Within a few weeks of each mailing, nearly every flight of 165 passengers was filled, most with long waiting lists.

Bingo.

The only group running low on numbers was the Cork Club in Houston. I called the secretary and scheduled a meeting with the club's owner. When I got into the taxi at the airport, the driver asked where I was going. As soon as I said "the Cork Club," the driver said, "Well, stay away from that owner, Glenn McCarthy."

"Why?" I asked.

"Taxi drivers won't pick him up anymore. He's always getting drunk and getting into fights and knocking guys out. He picks fights with everyone."

When I got there, I met with the manager. After 10 minutes or so, McCarthy sauntered into the room, looked me over, and walked back out. I didn't know how notorious he was. One of the most successful Texas oil tycoons, 59-year-old McCarthy had been on the cover of *Time* magazine, hung around with Howard Hughes and lots of Hollywood stars, and had even been the inspiration for the character Jett Rink in the book *Giant*—James Dean played his role in the resulting movie. He was known for being the picture-perfect stereotype of a big, bad Texas wildcatter oilman.

Afterward, people would ask, "You met Glenn McCarthy?"

"Well, I didn't exactly meet him," I'd say.

Two months before the first charter was set to take off, I took a quick trip to South America to begin making arrangements for our winter tours. Flying overnight from Santiago, Chile, to San Francisco via a Los Angeles stopover, I saw a passenger get on carrying the *Los Angeles Times*. On the front page in a red banner headline it said, "Red Guard Runs Amok in Hong Kong."

Oh, no, I thought. Not Hong Kong. Not now. If something were to go wrong, this was precisely not the time for it to go wrong. I was about to send 10 back-to-back charters to Hong Kong, and here we were at final payment time with stories of rioting gracing the front page of the newspaper.

On my arrival in Hong Kong, my agent met me at the airport and said, "You're staying at the Peninsula tonight on the Kowloon side instead of the Mandarin on the Hong Kong side. They've stopped the Star Ferry because the Red Guard is almost all the way down to the oceanfront."

The Peninsula hotel is gorgeous—one of the queen jewels of the world. That night, I stood behind glass doors with two fancily dressed guards. And just a few yards away outside, the Red Guards rolled over a car and set it on fire. That was as far as they ever got.

I flew back home with a terrible unease, wondering how I would manage if everyone canceled his or her trips. Miraculously, people didn't. We still had every charter sold out. Two days before our first charter was to arrive, I flew in early to do a "dry run." Everything seemed to be in place.

As an extra touch, I hired a junk to display a sign that said "Welcome, INTRAV Orient Adventure" for our passengers on their first crossing of Victoria Harbor.

The charter flew into Hong Kong, and the group got onto the Star Ferry. I looked for our sign . . . and nearly fell over. The junk was so close to the ferry that as soon as we took off, it almost got run over and swamped. I had to tell the guys, "Next time, would you please make sure you get out in front of the ferry and off to the side so my passengers at least have a chance of seeing the sign?"

But that was nothing compared to the bigger issue we were about to face: as we made our crossing, I looked down, and there was a dead body floating in the water. The Red Guards were killing people in Canton, and the bodies were floating down the river into Hong Kong Harbor.

The president of the organization, who booked the charter, saw the body and said, "I'm only a small-town doctor in Iowa, but I'm certain that's a dead body floating there."

I'll never forget those words. I was glad he took it so well.

Thank goodness the rest of the trip went off without a hitch. And thank goodness the Red Guard rioting ended in October.

The social norms in the Orient were so different from what our tourists were accustomed to. On a subsequent trip, we took our group to the annual Gion Festival in Kyoto, a colorful celebration in the geisha area downtown. It's punctuated by a parade every July 17 where women dress in kimonos and wave their paper fans and men wear traditional Japanese garb and play instruments or pull floats or chant through the streets. We always warned our clients to leave their valuables behind when traveling, but they didn't always listen. In this case, one of our clients had his passport, cash, and traveler's checks in his camera bag. He put his bag down when he was taking pictures of the parade, and when he turned to pick it back up, it had disappeared.

We were leaving Kyoto the next day to go to Hong Kong, so we put him in a car and raced him to the American consulate in Osaka to get him an emergency passport so he could leave with us. By the time he got back from Osaka, there was a message from the police: the crook had called to report his own crime.

"When I opened the bag and saw the passport, I realized I had stolen from a foreigner," he told them. "I know that would bring dishonor to my country, so I've left the bag in a telephone booth for you to pick up." All of the contents, including the cash, were still in the bag when the police retrieved it and gave it back to its owner. Honor among thieves, indeed.

Kyoto was also the first place where the mayor gave me the keys to the city. He appreciated that I was promoting tourism to the city and wanted to commemorate INTRAV's accomplishments. On this day, I was in the city with my first salesman, an older man with white hair who was also a friend of mine.

"Come on, Ken," I said. "Come with me. It'll be fun. You'll get to meet the mayor."

At the ceremony, the mayor was obviously looking at and heading for Ken with the key to the city. He assumed that the older guy with the white hair was the boss.

Ken looked at me and murmured, "What do I do?"

I put my hand on his back and said, "Go ahead and take it." We'd sort it out later—why embarrass the mayor?

When I got back home, I finally started sleeping again. For the first time in seven years, I really slept. I knew then that a bad year was going to be $3 million in revenues. No matter what your economic comfort level is, you can live on $3 million a year.

I felt the fear leaving my body. My family was never going to have the worries I did when I was a child. For the first time, I knew I'd achieved more than I'd set out to do. We'd already made history: no other company had ever done back-to-back charters before, and we'd just sold out 10 of them. Japan allowed only 30 charter flights from the United States annually, and by 1969, we were using all of them.

We were bigger than the big guys now. INTRAV was a stunning success.

Chapter Seven

MAKING
HISTORY

My "B or B" year had the right outcome. From that point on, I knew that I'd always have enough to support my family, which had been my goal from the start. All I'd wanted was stability, and now I had plenty of it.

Except for my Olympic dreams, I hadn't ever envisioned making history when I was a child. Now newspaper and television reporters were waiting at the airport to interview my passengers and me about these historic back-to-back charter flights, and government officials gave me awards commemorating the event. It was a big deal not only to me but also to the whole travel and tourism industry. We expanded the realm of what was possible.

Of course, I was not one to rest on my laurels, so I continued looking for ways to expand the company and its offerings. Just as competitive as ever, I wanted to do better every year. I marketed INTRAV heavily to several specialized groups: private clubs, dental associations, bar associations, and university alumni associations.

We tapped into the medical associations in 1968, which was a major coup. Medical associations turned out to be loyal; if you give them a great travel experience, they're not likely to feel the need to "shop around" next time they're ready for a new trip.

After successfully selling out 10 back-to-back charters to the Orient, I needed a winter product to sell. I'd just been to South America for the first time the previous winter with a senior golf tour, and I thought, "Why not South America?" I traveled there again in June to design the itinerary and hire the operators and decided on four days in Quito, Ecuador; four days in Santiago, Chile; four days in Buenos Aires, Argentina; and four days in Rio de Janeiro, Brazil. That started our second series of trips in January 1968.

Following that, I created tours for the South Pacific the subsequent winter: Tahiti, New Zealand, and Australia. Next came North and East Africa: Rabat; Morocco; Nairobi; Kenya; and Tunis, Tunisia. My plan was to produce a Rolls-Royce for the price of a Ford; no matter where we went, I wanted people to feel they were traveling in luxury without having to pay luxury prices. One of the biggest selling points was that they'd fly from their own local airport, without having to go through an international departure city.

Take the example of a well-to-do doctor in Texas. He's always encouraging his patients to take vacations for their health, but he's too busy to take one himself. His wife has always talked about going to Europe or Asia or South America, but Dr. Jones hasn't gotten around to it. He's not interested in sitting in a terminal in New York and wasting his vacation while being herded around like cattle by rude airport security guards, but if you can get him on a Texas Medical Association charter flight out of Dallas, then it's a different story. His wife gets her trip overseas, he gets a tax deduction for continuing education, and he's still Dr. Jones—with all the respect that entails—throughout the experience.

The wonderful thing about setting up new tours was that once I had all the details right, they were easily repeatable. It reminds me of the success of a friend who was an architect and developer. He was hired to design and build a small regional hospital. The design called for 150 beds, and he sold it for approximately $5 million. Then he thought, "I can sell this hospital all over the country"—and he could do it for $3.5 million instead because now he already had the plan. It brought down costs for his buyers, and he ended up making significant income building the same hospital all over the United States. Without knowing it then, we had both discovered one of the new innovations of the '60s: bundling the components into a more economical package.

In essence, I did the same with my charters. How do you hold costs down? By doing everything on a bigger scale and dividing the start-up costs among as many people as possible. That meant I had to find more and more people to trust INTRAV with their travel plans. Once people saw what we were able to accomplish, that wasn't hard. We had no competition in most markets.

The groups I worked with clamored for more destinations, so I traveled around the world to look for the best experiences and accommodations I could find. Whether people wanted to go on a big-game photo safari or surf on the most beautiful beaches, we would get them there.

"What would be better than a two-week air and sea trip to the Mediterranean?" I thought. I chartered the British ocean liner *Carmania* of the Cunard line, which had been out of service, and we did a series of two-week cruises. On the first trip, we flew to Nice, France, and I remember having two DC8s and a 707 at the airport, and Air France had just one 707.

"My gosh," I said to myself, "we're three times bigger than the national carrier."

We needed three planes because the ship carried 550 passengers. I liked to arrange trips where I'd "matchmake" the passengers; one cruise might consist of the members of Ohio Medical, Illinois Medical, and Texas Medical. Those were the first air/sea tours ever done, and they were right at the beginning of the cruise era.

A talent agency in England specialized in cruise ship entertainment, so I utilized its services to find our entertainers. We ended up with a typical cruise band and an aging dance team from Portugal: Philippe and Olga. They were past their prime, and she was in no shape for dancing anymore. The finale of their show was when he'd twirl her around in the air and then she'd stagger around the stage when he put her down.

In time for the next trip, I did a little recruiting of my own. I hired the Rumors, a local band in St. Louis that I thought was hip. They were white kids, but the lead singer, Corky, had an afro. I treated them like big stars, and they followed suit by acting the part. We pulled up to the Hotel Negresco in a limousine, and in front of the uniformed greeter, the singer slid out onto the sidewalk on his rear end. He looked up and slurred, "Bonjour, Monsieur!" I thought, "Uh-oh . . . this isn't good."

When we got to the ship, it turned out that the band's amplifiers hadn't shown up. I chartered a plane to fly all their equipment to Catania, Italy. We were all on the C deck, and Corky wrote "The C Deck Blues," which included lyrics about how the C deck had no private bathrooms.

Our agent in Sicily looked like Humphrey Bogart, and his son rode shotgun for him. He lived in the mafia headquarters city and was overqualified to be a tourist agent, but I didn't ask probing questions about that. Instead, I stuck to the more pertinent matters—and at the moment, the most pressing one was "Did the band's equipment arrive?"

"Yes," he said, "but I guess we should tell you . . . you just bought a dead horse."

"Excuse me?"

They explained that the truck carrying the equipment had arrived at the port but the dock manager informed them they weren't allowed to bring a truck on the dock.

"What are we supposed to do? This is heavy equipment, and the ship is at the end of the dock."

"Under the old law, you can take a horse-drawn wagon out there, but you can't take a truck."

"How are we supposed to get a horse-drawn wagon?"

"We have one we can rent you."

Well, that was convenient.

Now, this next part sounds like a cockamamie story to me that I was never inclined to verify, but what they told me was that the horse dropped dead while carrying the equipment down the dock. And I had to buy the horse.

After all this trouble, the Rumors had better be the best band my passengers have ever heard, I thought.

That night, the band played. Their specialty was "Proud Mary," and they amped everything up good and loud. When Corky got to "Rollin', rollin', rollin' on the river," they blew out every light on the ship, along with our navigation system. The Rumors were strutting around the ship like rock stars proud of their feat, and we were in an emergency situation.

I took them off the ship and flew them home and decided never to recruit entertainers again. What I've learned in the ensuing time is that people who manage musicians generally treat them like meat so their egos don't overinflate, and I'm just not a meat manager. We stuck to regular cruise line entertainers for the rest of the cruises, which were filled to capacity.

During our North and East Africa program, the Rabat Hilton where we stayed was nearly empty; it was at perhaps 15 percent occupancy and likely should have closed for the winter. I knew that what I had was a great bargaining chip: we were bringing in hundreds of tourists on a back-to-back basis for three months, and the hotel would not be able to fill those spaces otherwise, so I negotiated hard. Among other things, I got the manager to agree to a full American breakfast with bacon and eggs every morning for $1.23. Well, we got our $1.23 breakfast, but I did learn a lesson about driving too hard a bargain. I've never seen such small portions of eggs in my life.

Because of our tours, I got to know the minister of the interior of Morocco. After our program was over for the year, he contacted me in St. Louis and said, "The king wants to give you an award, and he wants you to come to his forty-second birthday celebration in June. We're going to send you an invitation."

He didn't explain what the award was, but I never received the invitation, so I didn't go to the party. That was rather fortunate, considering that was the year palace coup d'état occurred and rebels with machine guns opened fire on the party guests. The king survived, but my friend—who I'm sure I would have been seated next to—was killed, along with nearly 50 other guests. That was a party to miss.

The king knew only one person could be responsible for the attack: Morocco's defense minister, Mohamed Oufkir. Although it was officially reported that Oufkir committed suicide after the coup failed, his body was found with multiple bullet wounds.

The next year, the new minister called to tell me that the king still wanted to give me an award.

"Where?" I asked.

"At the Moroccan Embassy in Washington."

"Good . . . I'll accept it."

I never received the invitation, and I never got the award. But I also didn't get killed at the birthday celebration, which I think is a fair trade.

As our successes mounted, in 1969 I hired a vice president of operations, responsible for program planning and ground operations. Each year, we took on about 10 new employees, so we were up to about 40 at that point. Then I decided we should hire one more employee: my dad. He was 64 years old and still wanted to work, though he'd never really had a job he loved. He worked for a series of manufacturing companies that were poorly run. I said to him, "All my life, I've heard about these idiots you've worked for. Why don't you come work for me as our administrative manager? I'll double your salary, and you can tell me how stupid *I* am."

He did, and I learned a lot from him. He handled purchasing, printing, and the mailroom, and he oversaw the office. Dad had a vantage point different from mine and could see when things weren't being done properly on the lower levels. To be a good leader, you can't possibly do everyone's jobs; you have to hire wisely and then sit back and let people do their work. I knew that somewhere down the chain someone wouldn't be doing the job the way I would do it, but that's why I was the one running the company instead of the other way around. My dad provided valuable insights about where there were weaknesses in the organization and helped me learn more about delegating down instead of trying to do it all myself.

We had lunch together once a week, but aside from that, it was all business in the office. I took my job seriously and expected everyone else to take his or hers seriously, too—even my dad. Socializing was for weekends.

Dad had many great aphorisms. One of them was "I don't want to be a millionaire; I just want to live like one." I told him I could make sure of that for him, and I did—as much as his pride allowed. If there was one thing I could do well for him, it was to send him to some of the greatest places, with Rolls-Royces to pick him up and fancy suites to sleep in.

I thought it was a great idea when I offered to send him, along with my aunts and uncles, on a trip back home to England. His sister Muriel still lived there. Muriel was just a baby when my father emigrated to the United States, and I thought he would love to see her. However, about six weeks before they were to leave, my dad said with no explanation, "I'm not going." I think it was too traumatic for him.

So instead, I sent him on trips to Hong Kong every year. Considering I was the Mandarin Hotel's biggest customer, they were happy to put him in the Mandarin suite. They rolled out the red carpet for him and drove him around in a Rolls-Royce. I still knew that Dad was nostalgic about England, though, even if he couldn't bring himself to visit his home. That's why I got so excited when I found Christchurch, New Zealand, and realized how similar it was to where my dad grew up in Colchester. In fact, considering how much England had changed over the years, Christchurch looked more like my dad's Colchester than modern-day Colchester did.

"You have to see this," I told him. It was a perfect little city that remained rooted in its English past. The architecture, the gardens . . . it was like stepping right into a nineteenth-century

English town. The residents didn't lock their doors, and natural beauty abounded in all directions. My dad ended up visiting every year. It was his way of recapturing England without all the emotional baggage that came with going home again.

I was happy to have my dad so immersed in my everyday life and working alongside me, but meanwhile, Martine and I were growing frustrated because we still hadn't started the family we both wanted. I was ready to be a dad, and she was beyond ready to be a mom. We sought help with Masters and Johnson—which causes a bit of a laugh when I mention it nowadays, but before they were known for their sex program, they were fertility specialists. Bill Masters intimidated Martine terribly; he had eyes of steel and a demeanor to match, but he was a very smart scientist. Virginia Johnson was the hand holder with no degree who had originally been hired as Bill's research assistant. After they poked and prodded Martine and ran their tests on both of us, I turned to Bill Masters and said, "Lay it on the line for me. Why aren't we having kids?"

He said, "There's nothing wrong with Martine or you, but there's an X factor. Quite frankly, scientifically, we don't know why you're not having children."

I had almost accepted the possibility of a life without children of my own when, lo and behold, Martine unexpectedly got pregnant a year later. I was in the delivery room on November 22, 1969, watching when our daughter was born. Our marriage was troubled by then, and I knew we faced an unsteady future together. Yet here was this perfect little girl, just as we had hoped. We named her

Christiane, after Martine's sister. It seemed only fair, considering Martine's sister had allowed me to take her out on our first date on New Year's Eve.

Soon after Christiane's birth, INTRAV had outgrown our current office and moved to the high-rise Missouri Theater Building at 634 North Grand. The name was a bit of a misnomer, as no theater remained on site. The theater had been torn down in 1957 to create a parking lot for the office building.

Six months later, Martine had taken baby Christiane to Paris for a visit. When they returned, I went to the airport to pick them up when we spotted a familiar face walking toward us: Bill Masters.

"Look!" I exclaimed proudly, showing off my daughter. "The X factor!"

Martine was in her glory in her role as a mother, and I kept working as hard as ever to provide for the family. Our marriage split up when Christiane was 18 months old, but I saw her on the weekends. She was a delight then and became more and more important to me as she got older. We went to the zoo together and rode bicycles and did lots of fun father-daughter things.

I never did get the three daughters I had hoped for, but I often think of how close I came to not having any. The difference between three and one is nothing compared to the difference between one and zero. I am so lucky to have her and lucky that she grew up knowing that both of her parents love her very much. Martine is a wonderful mother, and I like to think I've done a good job as her dad, too.

In 1972, I offered to buy my parents their first house. They had been renting all their lives, and my mother was eager to have more space. I took her around to look at houses on the market. My aunt and uncle had moved to a newer area in northwest St. Louis, and Mom had her eye on a nice subdivision there.

I knew it was a touchy subject with my father, though—I had no desire to wound his pride or make him feel like I looked down on the life he had made for us. When you do things to help people, at what stage does it magnify the deficiency? And although he was proud of my business success, I knew it was a double-edged sword: my success could make him feel less successful by comparison. He was initially reticent about my offer, so I approached it in a more pragmatic manner.

I said to him, "You'll never have to ask a landlord again whether you can dig up the lawn to make a garden. You can do whatever you want. It'll be all your property to grow whatever kinds of flowers or vegetables you like."

That's what sold him on the idea. His family was full of avid gardeners. He and my uncle had kept a victory garden during the war. Dad loved the idea that he wouldn't have to ask permission to have whatever kind of garden he wanted.

They became homeowners for the first time in their late 60s, and my dad quickly took full advantage of his newfound freedom. I knew he had fully crossed over to his new lifestyle when I arrived at his house one day and found him sitting on the stoop in the backyard with a gin and tonic in hand, presiding over the young man he had hired to tend to his gardens. He was the lord of his land, and he clearly enjoyed his role.

"He's getting old. He's becoming a gentleman farmer," I thought. "But this is wonderful."

The backyard looked ridiculous. Whereas I've always liked a more controlled landscape, Dad just wanted to grow *everything*. He had roses and seemingly thousands of tomatoes and everything in between. The whole immense backyard was a giant garden, complete with compost piles: flowers on one side and vegetables on the other. It was wild and just what he always wanted. That was one of the happiest days of my life.

Now that Dad was retired, though, I got to see a new side of Mom. She had been the more subservient one, letting Dad rule the household. After his retirement, I heard her really let him have it once—and rightfully so. I'd never heard her yell at him before, and it made me uneasy. Then I realized what had happened: she was perfectly willing to let him rule the roost as long as he was gone for 40 or more hours per week, thus giving her plenty of breaks from him where she could be the queen of the castle. But now that he was home all the time, she could no longer stand for his domineering ways on a full-time basis.

I never heard her yell at him again, but I didn't have to. I knew that something had shifted, and as much as I loved my dad, a piece of me was proud of her for standing up to him at last.

One of my frequent stops on my travels was to visit my cousin Jean and her husband, Bob. Jean was an only child who moved to New York to be an actress and met up with Bob, who was then working for William Morris. He was a real character—brilliant and strange. Nobody in the family liked him except me. I knew he was a genius.

They ended up moving to Hollywood and never moving back East. Bob wound up in a position of power at every studio—either as a vice president or general manager at RKO, MGM, Paramount, and Universal. Among Bob's eccentricities was that he always wanted to live in the last house on a cul-de-sac "so nobody is above me."

One Tuesday morning while I was staying over at their new home, I awoke to the sound of sawing. I came out of my room to see what was going on and saw Bob still in his pajamas and slippers with a saw in his hand. He was hacking away at the door.

"What are you doing? That's your front door."

"Yeah, I know. I want the dogs to be able to come in and out."

He was making his own dog door for their Scotties. As usual, there was no stopping Bob when he was on a mission, so I just chatted with him while he wrecked the door. As long as it worked, he didn't care what it looked like.

After breakfast, I took a drive and noticed something strange. "I saw at least three or four new Cadillac convertibles and Rolls-Royces on your street, and there are guys out there washing them. What's going on?" I asked Bob.

"Oh, those are unemployed actors," he told me. "They made the money, and now they have the time."

That was often Bob's story, too. He'd run a studio for 18 months and then wind up unemployed for two years before picking up his next job. He got fired a lot—his higher-ups didn't put up with him for very long stretches, which I think is a common problem among geniuses. And that's what Bob was: a Brooklyn Jewish genius who didn't suffer fools and said what was on his mind. The fact that he was rough around the edges didn't make a difference to me; I admired him for his talent and intellect.

Every time I went to visit, I'd treat them to dinner because he was generally unemployed. During his down periods, he'd write treatments for screenplays, which I'd proofread for him. He really was a writer at heart, and his eccentricities stretched to his writing habits as well—he had a La-Z-Boy recliner that he liked to lie down in while he was writing, so he had to rig his equipment to work that way. He attached his typewriter to a table that he turned upside down so he could write flat on his back. Then he took apart the telephone and hooked it up to earphones so he could answer the phone if he needed to without getting up from his "writing space."

Jean would act in commercials, which brought in their only income for large chunks of time. She still looks 20 years younger than she is and has always been attractive. Although they didn't have any children, she usually played the mother in commercials. Commercial work is harder than it looks—the days can start at 3:00 or 4:00 in the morning and go all the way into the late-night hours, but it can also mean tens of thousands of dollars for one commercial, depending on how many times it airs. Aside from that, all they had were the unemployment checks that always ran out too soon.

Finally, Bob got a job with Jack Webb and brought back *Dragnet*, the TV police drama that Webb created and starred in. Webb took his research seriously and wanted *Dragnet* to represent the best about the police force, unlike the cartoonish or brutish ways police were often depicted in movies. He worked closely with the LAPD, and the shows often came straight from their files. As a result, Bob also developed close relationships at the police and fire departments.

Bob played a major role in publicizing the 911 telephone system for the Los Angeles fire and police departments, as well. He created the show *Emergency*, which was about emergency workers responding to calls. Bob's shows taught people what 911 was for and how to use it. As a trophy for his good work, he had police and fire chief badges for about a hundred cities throughout the United States. The greatest perk, however, was yet to come.

The next time he picked me up at the airport in his new Mark IV coupe, he said, "Look at this!" with an enthusiasm usually reserved for children.

Under the dashboard was the official LAPD and fire department radio band, and it accompanied one of the flashing red lights that can be mounted on top of the car.

"What do you know? For a kid from Brooklyn, you've died and gone to heaven," I said. "You can legally chase fire trucks and police cars and get paid to do it!"

When Bob died, the only family members to attend his funeral at Forest Lawn were my cousin, my wife, and me. His sister from Brooklyn canceled at the last minute. Nevertheless, the church was packed. One hundred fifty police officers and firemen must have been there, all in uniform. Both departments had shown up to pay their respects. Then, the actors he had worked with, many of them famous, gave the eulogy. David Hasselhoff was among them.

I had never watched much television—mostly, I just made myself stop working in time for the 10:00 news, and I liked *M*A*S*H* and *Kojak* at 10:30. To me, many shows seemed to have underdeveloped plots and wooden actors. Bob was the type of boss who never let that slide. He was a perfectionist who worked his actors and crew hard, demanding the best out of them. Of course, he probably treated his bosses with the same rough demeanor, which is why he got fired so often. But Jack Webb kept Bob in his employ for 10 years, until Bob retired.

One actor at the funeral service stood at the podium and said, "Bob was the best damn son of a bitch I ever worked for. My wife said I couldn't use these words in a church, but it's true."

Another actor said Bob had been the best father he'd ever had.

Bob's role in life became clearer to me that day. He was like the tough coach who matters to his players; he had a rough exterior, but he had done so much for their careers, and so many people respected him. I wished the family could have seen how much of an impact Bob had on people. It seemed a shame that they never knew.

My philosophy about life and relationships was different from Bob's. My family always remained very important and close to me, and I often did things for them before I did them for myself. I bought my parents a television before I bought one for myself.

When a girlfriend told me she wanted to marry and buy a house, I told her I could fulfill one out of two of those wishes; I bought her a house before I moved on. At that point, I was still just renting my own house. I hadn't yet figured out the emotional benefit of having a house that was truly my own.

I remained a competitive person regardless of whether anyone was standing at the sprinter's starting line with me waiting for the gun to go off. My goal was to sell out every flight. I communicated with my suppliers by giving them weekly booking records, something no one else did. Sometimes I fudged the reports a bit if I knew I had a promotion coming up—I didn't want them to worry that a trip looked empty when I knew that it would be full in two months, after our mailing went out.

Airlines nowadays often overbook flights, and we occasionally did that, too, but the difference was that we kept on top of our numbers and worked to keep everyone happy. "You don't cancel a passenger," I'd tell my sales staff. "You *finesse* a passenger."

The difference is simple: canceling a passenger means bumping a person from a trip because you overbooked it. Finessing is calling and offering the person a 50 percent discount to move to a trip leaving two weeks later instead. We always tried to do the right thing by our clients, and I'm proud that they recognized that.

There are many ways to run a travel company, but the model I built was to have the salespeople out in the field all week rather than making phone calls. They all lived in St. Louis and were generally in town on Monday for a sales meeting and back in town on Friday for a sales recap. In between, they were in their territory and were meeting with people.

In addition to the sales force, we had sales administrators who stayed in the office to talk to clients on the phone, as well as reservationists, a big marketing department, and a mailroom staff. Each year, we'd have a new crop of all-American escorts for our tours. Most of them were university honor graduates. The boys were football captains, and the girls were homecoming queens. Most were presidents of their fraternities or sororities. I was proud of the family we were building in the company.

As time went on, I continued introducing new tours: Scandinavia, Central America, and South Africa.

When I arrived in Kenya to prepare for the African Adventure tour in 1968, I was introduced to Dr. Julius Kiano, the minister of education and a very powerful man. He invited me to the fifth annual Independence Day celebration, marking Kenya's liberation from Britain. I had lunch with President Jomo Kenyatta, who was the George Washington of Kenya—its founding father—and Tom Mboya, the heir apparent. We watched all the tribes of Kenya dance. It was like being at a Fourth of July celebration in 1797, sitting between George Washington, John Adams, and Thomas Jefferson.

The next step in INTRAV's natural progression was to begin offering around-the-world chartered flights. We stopped in Honolulu, Sydney, Hong Kong, New Delhi, and the Serengeti.

We ran six of them one year; in fact, we were the first to do six around-the-world charters. We made history, and I made a wonderful profit. For a guy who just wanted to earn enough to get by, I had sure blown that out of the water. I was a millionaire many times over before I was 35.

Now that I was no longer the sole salesman and writer, I took on a role more like the one I had when I ran the NCO clubs: I would read the weekly sales reports, much like the consumption reports, and try to figure out where there might be problems. I heard every baloney story there was from the salesmen when their numbers were down—like the ones who'd tell me they mailed out brochures that they hadn't.

"We're at 80 percent capacity on the first two charters, the third one is full, and the fourth one is at 70 percent, but the fifth one isn't booking at all. So either the mailing didn't go out or we really have a problem," I'd say. Inevitably, the answer was that the mailing hadn't actually been made.

I made some adjustments to our tours as we saw what worked and what didn't. On our first year of the African Adventures, I booked four days in Morocco, four in Kenya, and four in Tunisia. Then I realized that there might not be enough to see in Tunisia in the winter to justify spending four days there. As an alternative, passengers could choose to fly to Rome and stay at the Hilton. Our escorts would arrange for side trips for our clients—golf, sightseeing, or anything else they could imagine. Everywhere we went we had a hospitality desk. At the Hilton in Rome was a big sign that said, "INTRAV African Adventure."

One day, Orson Welles swept into the lobby with his black cape and finally stopped in front of our sign and dramatically flung his cape around, saying, "African Adventure? Why doesn't somebody tell these people where they are?"

That hotel teemed with celebrities. Telly Savalas of *Kojak* fame played poker in the lobby every day with his entourage. Another time, I had a close encounter in the elevator at the hotel. Leaning against one side of the elevator was a very good-looking man, and leaning against the other side was a very beautiful woman. The two were making eyes at each other, so I went to the back of the elevator so as not to interrupt. I couldn't help but look at them because they were both so attractive, and finally as we arrived on the first floor I realized who they were: it was singer Robert Goulet making eyes at his wife, singer Carol Lawrence! I think I let out a gasp, and the two of them burst out in laughter.

The following year, I realized we needed more time in Kenya, so I took out Tunisia and made the trip six days in Morocco and six days in Kenya. It was the only program I ever radically changed.

Once again, all of our tours were sold out, and we sold them for $898. We flew from more American cities to more foreign destinations than any other airline or tour company—more than 100 cities across the country. As in track, my goal was to stay so far in front of everybody else that I didn't need to look over my shoulder to see who was coming up behind me. It worked a lot better in business than it did in track.

The next programs we did were multiples of cities in Europe. Among the itineraries were London, Paris, and Rome and Munich, Zurich, and Vienna by train. We also sold river cruises, which turned out to be big business. We were the first to do a Rhine-Danube cruise when those rivers were connected.

After our charter contract ran out for the *Carmania*, it was retired even though we had it filled to capacity for our Mediterranean cruises. Cunard just couldn't make it profitable. Like many others, it was an old ship and frequently in need of repair. They were made in the 1950s for transatlantic transportation, not leisure travel. In 1963 it was refitted as a cruise ship—but not very successfully. Many of the rooms were inside cabins, and they had only shared bathrooms and showers.

The next two years, we chartered the *Jean Mermoz* from the Paquet line. It was an improvement over the *Carmania* but still not the perfect vessel. It had also been built in the 1950s to take passengers and cargo from France to West Africa, and it was refitted as a cruise ship in 1969 because Greek and Italian shipping companies had created too much competition in the low-cost ocean liner marketplace for them. The refitting was more extensive than with the *Carmania*, but I still wished for something better.

"These ships are just barely acceptable," I thought. I wanted something I could charter that would provide the level of luxury my clients expected.

The next logical step didn't click into place until my accountant approached me with an enviable dilemma.

"You're making too much money," he said.

"Come again?" I asked.

By this point, we were so successful that our profits were millions of dollars a year in cash. I was paying 50 percent personal tax and 50 percent corporate tax. I would have paid myself the entire profit—$10 million a year—but Uncle Sam wouldn't let me. The government had rules in place to cap my personal earnings; I could pay myself only $2 million, and the remaining $8 million sat unused in the corporate account, subject to corporate taxes.

"If you don't do something soon, you're going to find yourself caught in 531, which is excess of surplus."

Section 531 of tax law code dealt with "accumulated earnings" and essentially meant that if my accumulated corporate earnings went any higher, I was going to have to pay even *more* taxes just for letting the money sit there. Talk about a disincentive to make money.

"So what do I need to do?" I asked.

"You have to find another use for your corporate cash."

I thought about what that could entail. Real estate is a great business, but I wasn't really interested in learning its ins and outs. It didn't take long, however, for the lightbulb to go off. *Wait a minute . . . I'm always looking for ships to charter. Why not build my own?*

That's how simple it was: necessity is the mother of invention, and in this case, I needed ships for my passengers. I also knew that cruises were the wave of the future; the cruise industry was off to a promising start, and I knew I could fill a niche in the market.

With that in mind, I started on my next business venture in 1972: the first Mediterranean cruise line, Royal Cruise Line.

Chapter Eight

CRUISING

Our first ship was the *Golden Odyssey*. My cruise director put me in touch with a Greek businessman who was looking for a project. We agreed to partner to convert an ocean liner. The original projected cost was $4 million, which then grew to $8 million and then $12 million. I finally said, "For this money, I might as well just build a new ship."

To do so meant that I was going to have to do something I had never done: borrow money. I didn't have a credit card, and I had never borrowed a penny. Zero. I bought all of my houses and cars with cash. If I didn't have the money for something, I didn't buy it. To build the *Golden Odyssey* would cost $20 million. I put up $4 million of my own and borrowed $16 million, guaranteed by the Danish government. That was my first loan: $16 million. "You might as well start with a big bang," a friend said.

I owned 98 percent of the company, and my Greek partner owned 2 percent in exchange for overseeing the new ship's construction and running ship operations in Greece. I then hired former travel agent Richard Revnes as president. He was an unbeatable sales and marketing man who'd end up gaining some fame in the industry for introducing gentlemen "hosts" onboard—middle-aged men whose job it was to dance with the single women and provide them with company during meals and excursions. It was actually Dick's wife's idea; she'd been on a cruise with him and suggested that he dance with some of the single women. Afterward, one woman generously thanked him for the company and told him she hadn't danced in years.

He then put out word that men who passed screenings and could dance well could get free cruises by fulfilling this role—which some laughed off as "geriatric gigolos"—but the idea ended up being adopted by many other cruise lines.

My strong business sense got our new venture off to a running start. I knew that every two weeks, Royal Caribbean took a charter load from Los Angeles on two-week Caribbean cruises, and Royal Viking was the new deluxe cruise line that was headquartered in San Francisco. They both had white yacht-like ships with a blue stripe running down the length of the ship, designed by naval architect Knud E. Hansen of Copenhagen. So I called Knud and had him design my first ship, white with a blue stripe, and called my company Royal Cruise Line. I moved into the building right next door to Royal Viking.

It was real chutzpah. The fellow who ran Royal Viking, Warren Titus, probably should have sued me. He didn't; he was such a gentleman.

The *Golden Odyssey* was a small ship for 460 passengers. The size was meant to match the capacity of a 747 so we could take the passengers out from our chartered plane onto our ship. We had a nice dining room, a theater and dance floor, an outdoor pool, a gift shop, and a small fitness center. It wasn't like the over-the-top cruise ships today that have three-story climbing walls, ice skating rinks with "Holidays on Ice" shows, three or four nightclubs with shows going on simultaneously, full casinos like the ones in Las Vegas, and so on.

I knew big money could be made in cruises—for one thing, they didn't pay taxes because they were operated offshore and their waitstaff was paid mostly in tips. I was watchful of what my competitors were doing. "If Royal Caribbean can market a two-week Caribbean cruise from California, I can do a two-week Mediterranean cruise. Mine's a better deal than theirs."

The *Golden Odyssey* went into service in 1974 and was an instant success. I had a built-in audience. For the first year, INTRAV chartered the *Golden Odyssey*.

Being a marketer, I knew that Royal Cruise Line could maximize sales on the West Coast and fill the *Golden Odyssey* on every cruise. That gave Dick Revnes one year to show the product to the travel agents of California, Arizona, Oregon, and Washington. European ship owners would put their U.S. office in either Miami or New York and market to the entire country. Every two weeks, we took a 747 load on a Mediterranean cruise starting at $898. I focused mainly on the California market, chartering one jet to fly from California to our various ports in the Mediterranean and then back again.

Just a few stumbles occurred because of the Greek staff, most notably on Thanksgiving. I got a call from our cruise director—who was formerly an American Episcopal priest who'd been living in Greece for 10 years—saying, "We need turkeys for Thanksgiving." So I gave him the go-ahead to order turkeys and then found out that he had served them a week early. He picked the Thursday before Thanksgiving.

Years later on an INTRAV cruise on the Danube, our cruise director told the Russian crew that we'd need turkey for Thanksgiving. "We don't know how to cook turkey," they explained—so our cruise staff cooked turkey for all the passengers.

Counting all the crew members of Royal, plus the U.S. staff in San Francisco, I now had more than 1,000 employees—and that didn't count the "extra" staff such as our headlining entertainers.

We often hired entertainers who were once very famous but whose careers had slowed down. They were excellent for our older clientele because the entertainers were most often the superstars of their youth. One of the most pleasant surprises was Rosemary Clooney, who became a great friend. On her birthday one year, she came to dinner at my house with her niece, and her niece sang for us.

I always thought it was amusing that when George Clooney first came to Hollywood, he would refer to himself as Rosemary's nephew, but when George's celebrity eclipsed her own, she referred to herself as George's aunt.

Barney and Muriel, 1936

University of Missouri— 100-, 220-, and 440-yard dash on track scholarship, 1954

Mom and Dad with Sing Shen, manager of Mandarin Hotel, Hong Kong, 1970

Christiane in fourth-generation communion dress, 1971

Barney and Marion and George Nakashima, New Hope, PA, 1973

Barney, 1973

Christiane and Barney, 1973

Bruna Panagoupolos and Barney at launching of MS Golden Odyssey,
first of three ships of Royal Cruise Line, February 1974

Christiane and Martine on Newport Clipper, 1983

Christiane,
1984

Christiane's graduation from Boston College, 1984

To Trish and Barney Ebsworth
With best wishes,

Ronald Reagan

Barney, President Ronald Reagan, and Trish, 1984

Eric Cantor, head of Christie's American sales; Barney; and Peter Rathbone, head of Sotheby's American sales, at opening of "The Ebsworth Collection," St. Louis Art Museum, November 1987: "Leave me alone, you've taken all my money!"

Barney and Emmy Pulitzer, with Joe Pulitzer in the background, December 1988

First and last ships Barney built (*MS Golden Odyssey*, Royal Cruise Line, and *MV Yorktown Clipper*, Clipper Cruise Line), Juneau, AK, 1990

Barney, 1991

Pam and Barney's wedding, with best man, Peter Ueberroth, 1992

Pam and Barney's wedding, 1992

Pam and Barney's
wedding reception,
Vouziers, 1992

Muriel and
Barney, 1992

Pam and Barney, Ginny and Peter Ueberroth, and Mary and Sam Cooke,
Barge Cruise, France, 1992

Barney, President George H. W. Bush, and Pam, 1992

Family cruise to Alaska on *Yorktown Clipper*, 1996
(front row: Jay Larimer, Pam, Muriel;
back row: Barney, Dave, two crew members, Pam's mom, Steve Larimer,
Jean Cinader)

Larry Johnson, Mary Cooke, Barney, Claire Johnson, and Sam Cooke,
African trip, March 1998

Pam, Barney, and Christiane at National Gallery of Art, Washington, D.C., *Twentieth Century American Art—The Ebsworth Collection*, March 2000

Jim Briggson, Barney, and Ted Christner at Seattle Art Museum, *Twentieth Century American Art—The Ebsworth Collection*, August 2000

Christiane and Mark's wedding day, October 2002

Barney and Martine at Christiane's wedding, October 2002

Christiane and Barney at her wedding reception, October 2002

Muriel and Barney at Christiane's wedding reception, October 2002

Isa D'Arleans, President George W. Bush, and Barney, 2004

Alexandra in
fifth-generation
communion
dress, 2006

The Ladds, 2010

Alexandra and
Maximilian, 2010

Ladd family, 2011

Barney's Old English Sheepdogs, Gen and Vanna, 2011

Each year, Rosemary would send me a Christmas recording. They were personalized messages: she'd start singing "White Christmas" and then break off in the middle of the song to talk to me.

"Oh, Barney, I haven't seen you in such a long time, and I miss you. We need to get together again soon . . ."

The messages were always sweet, and I finally gathered up all of them—about 10 of them—and put them on one recording so I could listen to them every Christmas.

A Boston-based travel company, American International Travel Service (AITS), was the only company doing back-to-back charters before INTRAV. They sold two-week tours that went from Honolulu to San Francisco to Las Vegas and back for $599. They sold like gangbusters.

As their second program, they chartered a ship called the *Theodor Herzl* for two weeks for South American cruises. I asked my operator whether he could get me onto the ship when it arrived in Rio de Janeiro, and he agreed. So, with one of my salesmen, I boarded the ship, along with the next group of passengers, trying to blend in. The boarding process was pretty disorganized—workers were still cleaning the rooms from the last passengers—so getting on the ship wasn't difficult. Once on, I was able to look around the decks and cabins, but I couldn't see any of the upper suites because the doors were all closed.

"Maybe the shades will be open in one cabin," I suggested to my salesman.

We forged ahead upstairs to find a window we could look into. Finally, we came to one with a shade that wasn't fully pulled down, so I bent over and stuck my face up to the glass to try to get a good peek at the room.

Inside was a woman getting dressed.

"Holy smokes. Let's get out of here!" I said to my salesman. "No one's going to believe I just wanted to see the suite."

We got off the ship as fast as we could before anyone stopped us for looking like a couple of Peeping Toms.

That wasn't my only "covert spy" mission gone awry. Shortly thereafter, I was in Istanbul and knew that a new Russian cruise ship was docked there. Russians had built four new cruise ships for their "hero workers" (also known as *Stakhanovites*, named for a man who had mined 14 times his quota of coal in a six-hour shift)—as an incentive, the government would take its best and most productive workers on pleasure cruises. This was mostly because watching people is easier when they're contained on a ship. There was too much risk if the government sent its best workers to Europe or Asia by plane; those workers may have disappeared and never come back to Russia.

One of my favorite operators, Omar Chaglar, seemed to be able to arrange everything in Istanbul, so I asked him, "Can you get me on the new Russian ship in the harbor?"

"Sure!" he said and proceeded to get me through customs and onto the ship. All the Russian passengers were sightseeing, and I went to the main lobby to look at the deck plan. There I was, alone, studying this map, when I felt the unmistakable presence of a very large person behind me.

"Vat you doing?" a Russian guard barked, pointing an AK-47 rifle right at me.

I had on blue jeans, a T-shirt, and tennis shoes and had a comb in my pocket but no wallet or passport or any ID.

"I'm sorry," I stammered. "I was just looking . . ."

"Get off this ship!" he yelled, and I complied as fast as one can comply with such an order. I got off that ship and berated myself the whole way. *Ebsworth, you are so stupid! You're in Russia illegally with no ID*. What would I have done if he had restrained me?

It was unsurprising to me that they had to work so hard to keep Russians in the Soviet Union. Because INTRAV was the largest producer of American tourists to the Soviet Union, I was given VIP treatment everywhere I went—and even that was not very good.

They booked me in Lenin's suite in the National Hotel in Red Square. The room had a couple of impressive oil paintings but not much else. The suite appeared not to have been changed or cleaned since Lenin had been there. It was filthy, and the bed was terribly lumpy.

Hey, I thought, *Lenin isn't buried in Red Square—he's still in this bed!*

In the hallway, workers rolled carts around noisily all night long, and you could forget soundproofing. It was like being in a hospital, where you can't get any sleep because of all the noise.

And I'm receiving VIP treatment. Imagine what it's like for every-one else in this hotel! I thought.

Guests didn't get keys to their rooms; you had to ask the "war-den" on your floor. They hardly looked like the welcoming sort. Dressed in what appeared to be prison guard uniforms, the tough-looking women would give you dirty looks as soon as you got near.

"Vat you want?" they would ask.

In my most timid voice, I'd squeak out, "May I have my key?"

The country was dismal, with fear integrally part of the cul-ture. On the subways, everyone had blank circles for eyes, like in the *Little Orphan Annie* comic strips. No one looked at each other, but in particular, people didn't look at foreigners or else the KGB might grab them. My company was proud to offer our clients the best hotels and best dining, but that wasn't saying much in a place such as Russia.

Restaurants in the country almost never had a menu. This was a place where people stood in line for five hours for a piece of meat for their family, only to get to the front of the line and find out there was nothing left. At restaurants, they'd bring whatever they had, and you ate whatever was placed on the table because you didn't know when or whether you'd be offered anything else.

When making arrangements, I had to speak delicately so as not to offend but still ensure that my guests' best interests were met. I met with the manager of the Leningrad Hotel and said, "We're going to have to serve lunch to 220 people tomorrow. Can you do that?"

"I'll show you," he said. "You be here at 11:00 and I'll show you your 1:00 lunch."

Sure enough, when I got there at 11:00 the next morning, there were eight round tables set with soup, entrée, and dessert, all sitting out ready to go two hours early.

It was possibly the most efficient thing about the hotel. Although the place was only two years old, nothing worked. The hotel had 11 elevator banks, but only two of them actually ran in this 20-story building. The manager proudly took me to my three-room suite, which boasted all gray furniture, gray walls, and gray rugs, with a picture of Lenin in one room and one of Brezhnev in another. The bathroom looked perpetually dirty, and a few feet away from the toilet was a circular hole in the floor. Oddly, it was stuffed with dirty rags. This was apparently meant to be effective camouflage, so hopefully you wouldn't notice the gaping hole incorrectly placed for the toilet plumbing.

Then, behind the bathtub was a closet—or at least, what purported to be a closet. It had a pole and hangers just like real closets do. The problem was that it had no floor and actually just led to the infrastructure of the hotel, so if you hung something in the "closet" and it fell, it was going to fall several stories all the way into the hotel basement.

I began wondering what we were so afraid of with Russia. Nothing worked in the country. It might have had a couple thousand fighter jets, but odds were that few of them could actually get off the ground.

Sometimes the worst trips were the most memorable.

I made a very big deal over our end-of-trip questionnaires. Every passenger would get one, and I thought it crucial that every passenger complete one. That way, no matter where I was, it was as if I was on every trip my passengers took.

I asked for feedback about every aspect of the trips: the airplane, the food, our crew, the hotel, dining, sightseeing, everything. Escorts announced at the beginning of the trip that the company expected them to return a completed questionnaire from all passengers and if there was anything unsatisfactory to let them know so they could correct it. "I'm here to satisfy you. My company expects me to return a questionnaire from everyone."

Maybe one in 500 passengers just couldn't be satisfied no matter how above and beyond you might go for him or her, but most passengers were reasonable. The escorts knew that destroying a questionnaire was a firing offense. They might get by once but not twice. Sooner or later, I'd hear if something was wrong. The system was wonderful for quality control.

We occasionally chartered from some of our friendly competitors, such as Royal Viking. I once said to Warren Titus, the president, "I know more about your ship than you do."

"How's that?" he asked.

"I get a 100 percent return of my questionnaires. Your purser is throwing away any reports that criticize him, but my passengers can say what's on their mind. I may not have as many reports, but I have 100 percent of the sample, and you don't."

People were surprised how serious I was about the questionnaires. After trips, I would follow up with any passengers who hadn't returned one. I'd write, "Thank you for taking a trip with us. I hope you had a wonderful time. I'm sorry that we haven't found your questionnaire. Would you please mail it to us as soon as you can?"

I really did want to know whether anything was unsatisfactory so I could make changes. In a business as competitive as ours, maintaining an excellent reputation and attracting repeat business were important to our success. We did that.

Meanwhile, my friend Ted Arison was not feeling so lucky. Ted was a very upbeat guy. He was an Israeli who became an American citizen, and he had cofounded Norwegian Cruise Line. After a falling-out with them, he and a partner went on to found their own company, Carnival Cruise Line. His first ship was a converted ocean liner originally built for the Canadian Pacific Steamship Company. He paid $6.5 million for it, renamed it the *Mardi Gras*, and had it repainted red, white, and blue. It could hold 906 passengers and would have round-the-clock activities and entertainment: the first "Fun Ship."

For the ship's maiden voyage, Ted invited 300 of the country's most prominent travel writers and travel agents to come aboard for a free trip out of Florida. It ran aground on a sandbar before they even left Miami, leaving the ship high and dry for a day and a half.

Shortly after that, I saw Ted, and for the first time I saw him look anything but happy. With his head in his hands, he told me, "I'm going bankrupt. My cruise ship ran aground at the worst possible time. You have a brand new ship, and you're doubling your equity every year. You're the big winner."

"No, Ted," I said. "You're going to be the big winner. Your Miami competitors are just ship owners, but you are a marketer." I knew it then, before he ever made his fortune.

Today, Carnival dominates the cruising industry. After buying up several other cruise lines, it now has a fleet of 101 ships.

One of Ted's assets was his ability to change with the times, a strength we shared. Every 10 years, I reinvented the company—not because I was bored and wanted change but because I was very good at looking over the next hill and figuring out where we were going to need to be in a couple of years.

For instance, we had started as a little travel agency selling individual plane tickets and tours, but I'd changed our direction until we were only chartering airplanes. We operated this way from 1967 until 1978.

Then came the deregulation of the airline industry. The Airline Deregulation Act was a federal law enacted in 1978, and it meant that the government would no longer set the rates, routes, and schedules of commercial airlines. Prior to that point, the Civil Aeronautics Board had to approve any new routes, fare changes, and schedule changes, as well as enforce the rules about who could charter a plane and under what circumstances. It was beneficial to large airlines, but passengers didn't appreciate the high fares and lack of competition in the marketplace.

Over the next year, the entire industry changed—airlines came up with a lowered group fare that made it impossible to take advantage of the economies of chartered flights. Rather than clinging to the model that had worked for me for the past 12 years,

I again reengineered our business. In 1979, 100 percent of our air travel was on chartered flights. In 1981, 100 percent of our air travel was on scheduled flights, and we expanded to include a large transportation department. Adapting to the market was one of my biggest keys to success.

I sold the majority share of Royal Cruise Line to Greek interests in March of 1979, which was the same year that I started Windsor, a company to provide financing for venture capital and real estate investments. I named the company after Windsor Castle, where my dad was born. Once again, my accountant had warned me that I needed to find a way to invest my corporate profit or risk being taxed at a higher rate for letting it sit there. It was a government penalty for accumulating too much cash and not investing it.

Windsor first invested in real estate: apartments, shopping centers, and office buildings. Then we decided to buy companies: a private-label shampoo manufacturer, a printing company, a manufacturing company, and a storage company, among others. I didn't run any of the companies; my role was strictly as an investor, not a hands-on manager. I hired a corporate CFO who managed the presidents of each company.

Over the course of 15 years, we didn't have any spectacular success. It proved to me that the management books are right: if your heart isn't in it, a business is not likely to be run very well. My heart was in none of these companies. They were just investments, and I had no personal connection to any of them. In the end, after all that work, we probably earned about the same amount we would have if I'd just left the money in the bank to earn interest.

On the other hand, I started another business that *did* mean something to me. In 1981, I founded another cruise line: Clipper. This time, I aimed smaller. These ships would have capacities of just 100–140 passengers, but they would be deluxe exploring ships with generously sized cabins meant for an upscale market. Over time, our fleet included the *MV Newport Clipper*, *MV Nantucket Clipper*, *MV Yorktown Clipper*, *MS Clipper Adventurer*, and *MS Clipper Odyssey*. Unlike Royal Cruise Line, this time I didn't limit myself to a particular geographic area: Clipper would travel far and wide, wherever our clients wanted to cruise in a more intimate manner than on the modern cruise ships. It was perfect for affinity groups, our specialty. Building the fleet also involved less of an up-front cost.

With small vessels such as ours, we could get into more secluded areas and offer more personalized service for our guests. Because of the size, our ships could maneuver into more delicate ecosystems and historic locales. Despite the fact that we were barely on the map in terms of the numbers of passengers we transported, we quickly gained a stellar reputation, eventually being named in *Condé Nast Traveler* magazine as one of the world's top 10 cruise lines.

Our offerings were diverse: we sold 20 unique itineraries across the waterways of North America from March through November each year, but that was just the beginning. In South America, our expedition vessel *Clipper Adventurer* carried people through the Orinoco and Amazon Rivers, as well as into Brazil, Uruguay, Chile, and Argentina. The same ship took passengers to explore from Greenland to the Northwest Passage, stopping just 155 miles away from the magnetic North Pole. We also offered trips to visit the Faroe Islands, Iceland, and arctic Canada.

Few passenger vessels could offer in-depth cruises in Antarctica, but *Clipper Adventurer* had an ice-hardened hull that was strong enough to handle the terrain, so we took people on 15- to 23-day trips to explore the geological formations and get up close with penguin colonies.

In the winter months, our *Newport Clipper, Nantucket Clipper, and Yorktown Clipper* offered week-long "yachtsman" cruises in the U.S. and British Virgin Islands or the West Indies, focusing on little-explored islands and coves that big ships couldn't access. Many of the spots we visited were tourist free except for us, leading to a different sort of experience than you'd get on the large cruise vessels. Rather than lounge acts, we'd have guest lecturers such as marine biologists and geologists.

We also offered six itineraries in the South Pacific with *Clipper Odyssey* to explore areas such as Australia's Great Barrier Reef, New Zealand's North and South Islands, and Papua New Guinea, along with numerous programs in the Far East.

Each new season, I enjoyed meeting our new employees.

"Please remember our first commandment: thou shalt not fraternize with your fellow crew members."

I'd look around the room and notice the solemn expressions.

"And remember our second commandment: thou shalt not get caught."

I knew it was going to happen. I just didn't want it affecting their work. So what I told them was that they were about to work harder than they ever had in their lives—12-hour days were the norm. If they wanted to go out and party for six hours a night, that was their business, as long as the next morning they were ready to put in another 12 hours with a smile.

And whatever they did, it worked. I'm very proud of the staff we built. The comments and reviews we received almost always mentioned how personable the crew was.

In addition to our Clipper offerings, INTRAV continued to do air-only tours, and we also chartered riverboats around Europe.

I had a particular fascination for the supersonic Concorde since it was first introduced for commercial flights in 1976. It was a joint venture of the British and French governments because of the formidable start-up costs for manufacturing and testing. Its makers promised that the planes would fly at twice the speed of sound—and they delivered. Reaching speeds of 1,330 miles per hour meant that passengers would get to their destinations more than twice as fast as when they flew on 747s. You could fly from New York to London in just over three hours. The record was two hours, 52 minutes, and 59 seconds.

It's like a magic carpet ride, I thought. I couldn't wait to try it.

Along with the increased speed came significantly increased fuel usage, which drove ticket prices out of the range of most passengers. These 100-seat aircrafts fell mostly into the purview of celebrities, wealthy businesspeople, and the like. Still, I knew some of our clientele would love the chance to try out the Concordes, and I set out to charter them. In 1987, we introduced a program called "Around the World by Private Concorde." In the following 12 years, there were only 30 around-the-world charters by Concorde, and 29 of them were ours.

The remaining one was a tour hosted by William S. Buckley. When it arrived in Sydney, Australia, missing a piece of its tail, which had broken off during the descent to land, reporters were at the airport to interview Buckley, but they also spoke to passengers, asking, "How did it feel when the tail broke off?" They couldn't find anyone who was even aware it had happened. That night on *The Tonight Show*, Johnny Carson said, "That's because Buckley was lecturing to them and they were all asleep."

I flew on the first around-the-world Concorde flight, and in a bout of serendipity, the head stewardess was named Martine and her assistant was named Christiane. We flew seven stops around the world and stayed at the best hotels and ate at the best restaurants, but the meals we ate on the plane were the best of the whole trip. The vice president of operations for Air France flew on the Concorde with us and had three days to get the meals ready for the next leg of the tour. We kept the same French crew throughout the trip, and they did a spectacular job. As usual, I made all the sightseeing trips available free for the crew; I wanted them to feel included so they'd have something invested in our group.

We departed from San Francisco and had to make our first stop in Honolulu for fuel because the Concordes burned fuel so quickly. I called my best friend Sam Cooke, who lived in Honolulu, and said, "I have two surprises for you."

"From the sounds in the background of your telephone call, the first is that you're at the Honolulu Airport. What's the second one?"

"I was in San Francisco two hours ago!"

A new speed record (that still stands).

It became evident that the Concorde industry wouldn't survive, however. The economics just didn't work. Even at the high rates they charged for fares, they couldn't make a profit. Redesigns were attempted; they thought about increasing the passenger capacity of the planes, but that would make the planes even heavier and less fuel efficient, requiring even more stops for refueling.

No new Concordes were manufactured after 1980, and some of the existing ones were retired and kept around for spare parts for the handful that were still flying. Before the end, Concordes were operating at far less than capacity and the airlines had to offer steep discounts to fill the planes. I'm glad to have gotten a chance to experience this piece of history.

Indeed, it was a wonderful period during which to live and work in travel. I had such a good time in business, aside from the plane crashes, terrorism, fires, earthquakes, tornadoes, shipwrecks, and explosions. Other than that, great fun.

I had considered at the onset of my entry into the travel business that some disasters were bound to occur along the way, but I did some interesting math and decided that I'd have to be in the business for 2,000 years before one of my planes would go down. And I didn't intend to be in business for 2,000 years, so I was safe.

Unfortunately, it didn't work that way. The worst disaster of my career happened on March 27, 1977, and a series of problems led up to it.

First, a bomb exploded in the terminal at Las Palmas Airport in the Canary Islands, which is where Royal Cruise Line's chartered Pan Am 747 was scheduled to land that day. Our flight, along with many others, was diverted to Tenerife Airport after the bomb exploded because a terrorist group warned civil aviation authorities that a second bomb was coming. So instead of landing in Las Palmas, our pilot was sent to land at Tenerife Airport. It was a small airport with only one runway, and now all incoming flights at the larger airport were being sent there.

Another Boeing 747 from the Dutch airline KLM landed at Tenerife before our plane did. That pilot—who was KLM's senior pilot and the guy they turned to when they wanted a pilot to give interviews on behalf of the airline—decided to do a complete refuel while he was waiting for clearance to go back to Las Palmas, to save time. Regulations state that he should have taken on only as much fuel as he needed for his next stop, in order to keep the plane's weight down for takeoff, but he took on 55 tons— enough to get him all the way back to Amsterdam. The refuel took about 35 minutes, and during that time, the Las Palmas Airport reopened for incoming flights.

Just before 5 p.m. local time, the KLM pilot asked for, and received, permission to taxi. The controllers instructed him to taxi to the end of the runway, make a 180-degree turn, and wait for permission to take off. During the refueling, however, a thick fog had set in and the runway had practically no visibility. The controllers couldn't see the planes, and the pilots couldn't see the other planes. No one should have taken off in these conditions; however, the KLM pilot wanted to get on with his flight and get back to his kids. He knew that if he waited much longer, the fog might get even worse and air traffic controllers would order him to stay on the ground at this unfamiliar little airport. His tone on the recordings betrays his impatience to get in the air.

What he didn't realize was that our plane was taxiing on the runway. The KLM pilot asked for permission to take off and got a nonstandard answer that was unclear. They said, "You are NOT cleared for takeoff." It included the word "takeoff," so the pilot wanted to believe he was clear—but controllers hadn't given clearance and were telling KLM to wait. "We're going!" the pilot said, emphatically overriding his copilot's questioning about whether the Pan Am plane was on the runway. "Oh, *yes*," he said dismissively.

KLM barreled forward at top speed, and the Pan Am pilot was heard saying, "Damn, that son of a bitch is coming straight at us!"

He tried to move the plane out of the way but was unable to maneuver in time. The planes collided at 290 miles per hour. KLM's pilot had tried to take off over our plane but couldn't and knocked straight through the Pan Am, taking the top of the plane off. In its wake, it sprayed all 55 tons of fuel over the plane and the runway and ignited multiple explosions and set the cabin on fire. The KLM 747 crashed and exploded.

Two hundred thirty-four passengers—most of them Dutch families, including 54 children—and 14 crew members had all died.

Our group hadn't fared much better, but we did have survivors who were fighting to find a way off the plane and safely onto the ground. Most of our passengers died by fire, not by the impact. Twenty percent of the people were still alive, and for 20 minutes, they wondered why the firefighters weren't coming to help them. The airplane was collapsing in on itself, and the engines were disintegrating and throwing off metal debris. One flight attendant managed to pull a door open before she died. People climbed over seats to get out the door and onto the wing before jumping all the way down to the runway, sustaining injuries and dragging each other away from the burning plane. The survivors were taken to a nearby hospital primarily by taxicabs that had arrived on scene.

It was the worst accident in aviation history. In total, 583 people died, which was twice as many deaths as the previous worst aviation disaster. One of my vice presidents in California called me on the phone and said, "Did you hear about the Pan Am crash in Tenerife? I think it's our plane."

"No, can't be our plane," I said. But what would a Pan Am 747 be doing in the South Atlantic? It had to be a charter plane, and who would have chartered it except for us?

Even as the details emerged, I wanted to stay in denial. Everything that could have gone wrong that day had gone wrong;

if even one detail had changed, all those people might have been alive. *Had it been any day other than a Sunday, ours would have been the only plane on that runway*, I thought. *Why did it have to be a Sunday, the biggest day for charters?* Plus, there were only two air traffic controllers at work in Tenerife on that Sunday, and they weren't used to dealing with big jets and so many aircraft at once.

If only the KLM pilot hadn't refueled . . . if only the fog had lifted . . . if only there had been another runway, if only . . .

The disaster hit me hard on every level. A week later, I was named in the biggest lawsuit in history: $2 billion. The lawsuit was against Boeing, Pan Am, KLM, the Spanish government, and Royal Cruise Line. Of course I had nothing to do with the crash, but I spent three months waiting to be released from the suit.

On an emotional level, though, there was no "getting out." It was so painful to think about and to feel responsible for putting those people on that plane. Even though on a logical level I knew nothing I could have done would have prevented what happened, I took it very badly then and still do. Realizing that it was our plane and seeing the images of the wreckage on television were the lowest moments I can remember.

Those were far from the first deaths we'd experienced among our passengers, but the others were of natural causes, which gave me a wholly different feeling. Of course it was sad anytime someone died, but people had heart attacks and strokes and all sorts of other things on our trips, just like they do in everyday life, and I could accept that. When someone teased me that we must be killing people off on our trips, I had my accountant run some averages for me. It turned out that the average age of our clients was 72 and the number of them who died during the two weeks they toured with us was significantly lower than the statistical average of how many people of that age "should" have died in any given two weeks.

"Oh! Then you're keeping them alive," he said. Well, not exactly. The truth is that we had healthier stock than most average senior citizens. Sick people don't normally take trips.

In November of 1989, we sold Royal Cruise Line to Norwegian Cruise Line. I began to realize that you had to build much larger ships to stay competitive. This wasn't the business we had started 17 years earlier. We were a "boutique" line, and the business was becoming "Las Vegas." The cruising business was really only 20 years old by that point, and already we either had to get much bigger or sell out—so we took the second option.

By that time, Royal Cruise Line had three ships: *Golden Odyssey*, *Royal Odyssey*, and *Crown Odyssey*. The new owners closed Royal and rebranded the ships.

Clipper Cruise Line remained solely mine from 1981 through 1997, at which point I sold it to INTRAV. The ships were too small to make a great profit, but we were the only small cruise company making any money, and it all had to do with marketing. To make it in the small-ship business, you had to market like crazy. That, of course, was my specialty.

I had five operational companies and a corporate CFO, and a friend asked me, "How are you doing?"

"Great!" I said. "I have five of the best presidents anybody ever had and a great corporate CFO."

"You must be a business genius," he said.

"No, if I had done it the first time, I would have been a business genius."

Anyone who claims never to have made a hiring mistake isn't telling the truth. Résumés don't tell the whole story; someone may dazzle you with perfect credentials, but as you work with the person, you discover some fatal flaw. So part of being a successful businessperson is recognizing these mistakes, getting rid of people who don't fit with the mission, and finding the ones who do. Eventually, I got it all right.

An important principle I tried to impart on all my employees was that people just want to be *recognized*. No matter who they are or what they do, they all like to hear that someone appreciates them.

"I know a lot of people who can buy anything they want, but what they can't buy is recognition," I would tell the agents. So aside from offering the best trips at the best price, what we needed to do differently from the bigger companies was offer a personal touch.

Around the office, we had a favorite passenger—a woman named Grace from Iowa who traveled with us 38 times over 20 years. What I wanted the agents to do was make conversation the next time she called. "Is this Grace from Des Moines? You just returned from South America, didn't you? How did you like it?" The introduction of computers in our workplace made this so much easier. No longer did we have to search through thick files; we could pull up someone's history in a moment and see every trip he or she had taken with us. People may have realized that we were reading on a screen and not just remembering every detail, but that's OK. Recognition is still recognition, and it turned the conversation from a business transaction into a friendly chat.

It's a quality that our passengers also valued in our cruise directors. *Cruise Travel* magazine described one of Royal Cruise Line's cruise directors, whose full name is Fernando Duarte Nunu Batista Canillas Tarrapa Barrosa de Oliveira, as "probably the most personable cruise director afloat" and noted that "his uncanny ability to remember names is phenomenal." Indeed, he strove to have every on-board passenger's name memorized by day two of each cruise.

That's something people value and remember. Twenty years after she took her second cruise with us, one woman still marveled that the director remembered her name from a cruise she'd taken with us a few years prior. That was one of the things that set us apart and kept our customers so loyal.

I'm very proud to know that we enriched people's lives by introducing them to new sights, cultures, foods, and experiences they might otherwise never have dreamed of. I enjoyed scoping out these places myself and imagining how our passengers would feel when they landed and took in a new piece of the world's beauty. I was always interested in hearing about which places people liked best.

As for me, I'll still take Paris every time.

Chapter Nine

BRINGING THE
MUSEUM HOME

"Barney Ebsworth rode his bike from South St. Louis to the art museum and dreamed of being a great collector as a child."

That's what my friend Charles Buckley wrote in the initial draft for the catalog of my first art show. I couldn't believe my eyes when I read it.

"Charles," I said to him, "I dreamed of making $12,000 a year and supporting a middle-class family." Art collecting was nowhere on my mind as a child. My motivation was economic security, and my guess is that the majority of people who've wound up wealthy had similar motivation. The real gift in growing up without economic security is in seeing both sides of life—if you're born with a silver spoon in your mouth, you never know what it's like not to have a spoon. How can you ever fully appreciate what you have if you've never known what it is not to have it?

I made my money in the travel business while learning about art, history, and culture. If I'd amassed wealth in the iron and steel business, what would I have known about culture? I learned about the finer things in life while making my money. I feel very fortunate to have lived in two generations: the one that made the money and the one that learned how to spend it with a little dignity.

My bicycle museum adventures were Charles's imagination at work. My real interest in art didn't start until 1957, when I visited the Louvre every Saturday. I didn't give much consideration to owning art until I realized I had the money to buy it. I was spending only 10 percent of my income, so there was a lot of surplus. After making a few investments, I said to myself, "There's no reason I can't own pictures."

Nobody starts as a collector. You buy a few things you like, and then eight or 10 items in, someone says, "Boy, you have a great collection," and then you realize you have a collection.

In the beginning, I bought seventeenth-century Dutch art because that's where I felt comfortable. The first was a landscape I acquired in London. To buy something, I wanted first to make sure I understood the artist, liked the piece, and knew it was one of the artist's best works. In real estate, they say three things matter: location, location, location. For me, collecting art was about quality, quality, quality. I would much rather have a smaller collection of the finest pictures than dozens of so-so ones.

Over a two-year span, I amassed a small group of seven Dutch pictures. I also collected a few Japanese scroll paintings from the late eighteenth and early nineteenth century. I had no real plan; I just bought the pictures that I thought were the best and that I could afford. I felt like I was bringing a piece of the museums home.

Then one day in 1971 as I was getting into the cruise business, the owner of the Holland America line invited me to Rotterdam for dinner. I'd never met him, but he was kind enough to invite me to his home—the Dutch are very welcoming that way.

"You're obviously a workaholic," he said. "Do you have a hobby?"

"As a matter of fact, I collect seventeenth-century Dutch art."

"Oh! Then would you like to see my uncle's collection?"

He handed me a book about the collection so I could be prepared, and then he offered to pick me up the next day to take me to see it. What I saw there astounded me—I walked out of there believing that the man had 15 Rembrandts, 27 Frans Hals, and his own museum and that it was hopeless for me ever to try to amass such a collection. When I went to visit the Boijmans Van Beuningen museum years later, I realized that my memory was exaggerated, but it was still enough to change my course. I was never going to own the best of the old masters paintings—they just weren't available, and the few that were had price tags I wasn't prepared to meet. To top it off, the field was already filled with so many experts that I knew competing with their expertise would be difficult when I didn't read, write, or speak Dutch and couldn't do the original research.

When I got back to St. Louis, I sat down with Charles Buckley, then director of the St. Louis Art Museum, to ask for his recommendations.

"I want to start collecting seriously," I told him.

"What do you want to collect?"

"Northern and Southern Renaissance—the Quattrocentro," I said. Even as I said it, I knew it wasn't possible.

"You spent a lot of time in Paris. What about the School of Paris—Picasso, Matisse?" he asked.

"I can't afford it." At the time, I was thinking in terms of $25,000 a picture, and the ones I would want were sold for more like $100,000 to $200,000.

"What about Impressionism?"

"I can't afford that, either."

"What about American Impressionism?"

"What is it?"

"Or how about American modernists or the Ashcan School?"

After a bit of discussion, that's where I settled. The artists of the Ashcan School were early-twentieth-century American painters who often painted ordinary New York City scenes. Robert Henri founded the movement and attracted four Philadelphia newspaper illustrators to join him in its core group: William Glackens, Everett Shinn, George Luks, and John Sloan. The "Ashcan School" name came from a critic who was insulting their work, but it stuck. I thought the pieces were interesting. "Let's try it," I said.

"If I see something coming up at auction that I think is of high quality, I'll bring it to your attention," he said in his typically understated fashion.

"I'm going to act as if I'm the curator of the St. Louis Art Museum—I'm going to buy as if I'm buying for the museum. I'm going to buy only the best and only what could hang on the museum wall right now, not sometime in the future."

One of my rules was to collect art by artists who were deceased, and that was for two reasons: First, I wanted to see the artist's whole range of work so I could pick out the work done at the artist's peak. Selecting work by living artists was like trying to hit a moving target. Second, I wanted my collecting to be about the objects and not about the artists; that is, I didn't want my feelings about an artist's personality to influence my judgment of a picture. I didn't want to meet the artists or learn about their personal lives. All that mattered was what I could see in the piece and how well I understood it in comparison to the artist's range of work.

After a couple of months, Charles called and said, "I want to show you something." When I arrived, he showed me the auction catalog for Parke-Bernet Galleries, predecessor to Sotheby's. In it was the William Glackens 1914 painting _Café Lafayette (Portrait of Kay Laurell)_. The picture was a beautiful woman sitting with a cocktail in her hand in what appeared to be a French restaurant. It had a Renoir-like styling that appealed to me. What made it more interesting was that eight years earlier, Charles had done the only retrospective Glackens ever had, making him the world authority on Glackens. If I were to trust someone's judgment on a Glackens picture, it would certainly be Charles's.

"The auction is next week. What do you want to do?" he asked.

"I'll get us two tickets to New York. Let's go look at the picture."

We did, and as we entered the room where the picture was situated on the far wall, I fell in love with it instantly.

"I'm going to buy this picture," I told him.

The subject of the painting, Kay Laurell, was an American actress in the early 1900s who was considered one of the prettiest showgirls to appear in the Ziegfeld Follies and certainly the sexiest: she appeared in the show in 1918 with her costume draped to expose one breast, meant to represent "the spirit of France." A fellow showgirl wrote in the book *The Days We Danced*, "Hers were the most exposed breasts on Broadway in that era."

William Glackens used her as his model several times. Years later, his son told me, "Kay was my father's mistress."

Charles and I walked around the gallery and looked at everything else, and at one point, he said, "Turn around and look at this picture. Here's an artist you should pay attention to also."

It was Charles E. Burchfield, an artist I'd never heard of. The frame was in bad condition, and parts of the painting were peeling, but it was a very interesting watercolor. I liked that it was somewhat surreal, which was unusual for American painting, particularly in that era.

It was a picture of two dilapidated houses and their snowy yards, but to me, it looked like two alcoholics who had been sleeping in an ash pit overnight; one was waking up, and one was still asleep. The anthropomorphism evident in the houses was striking.

When we returned home, I was still thinking about the Burchfield painting, but I knew nothing about the artist. I went to the library and found one book written about him, plus an article in another book. That's all that was written at the time. He painted almost exclusively in watercolor and often reworked his paintings after they were "finished." This painting, *Black Houses*

(The Bleak Houses), was featured in the book, and in my hour-long crash course, I decided that it was painted during his best period and that if the painting was in my range, I would buy it.

I went back for the auction and bought both pictures. Charles had asked me to call him and let him know how the auction went, so I called.

"I bought the picture," I told him.

"Good!" he said. "That's a good start. I'll see you when you get back."

"Hold on . . . I bought something else."

"What?"

"The Burchfield."

"Good for you!"

The Burchfield is in my bedroom now, and the Glackens is in the living room. At the next auction, I bought three pictures. One was Charles Sheeler's watercolor *Classic Landscape*. To me, Sheeler was the greatest precisionist painter and was not yet properly appreciated.

Sheeler was both a photographer and a painter. When the Ford Motor Company was preparing to unveil its new Model A, *Fortune* magazine hired Sheeler to photograph the River Rouge manufacturing plant near Detroit, Michigan. When he was finished photographing, he began painting—his paintings are inspired by the photographs but are not meant to be accurate reproductions. Sheeler's greatest precisionist picture was his 1931 oil painting *Classic Landscape*, which belonged to Mr. and Mrs. Edsel Ford. They bought it the year it was painted. I figured I could never own that piece, as they would certainly will it to the Detroit Institute of Arts, but there was a watercolor version of it that Sheeler had painted in 1929, and this is what was up for auction. At least I would have the image of the greatest precisionist picture.

Then I bought two more small paintings: a Stuart Davis and an Albert Bierstadt. In those days, after an auction ended, buyers would have to stand in line to sign a document stating what they'd purchased. There were two lines at the end of this event, and a friend of mine from Atlanta was in the other line across from me. When I got to the front of my line, I read the document that stated what I was buying: "Charles Sheeler: *Classic Landscape*; Albert Bierstadt: *Western Landscape*; Stuart Davis: *French Landscape*."

"My gosh," I said. "I bought three landscapes, and I wasn't aware I bought even one!"

A lady standing behind my friend in line said, "Somebody had better help this man!"

It was such a great comeback to an honest statement—I then realized I was concentrating on the object exclusively, not the category or the title.

The following day, I walked into Kennedy Galleries, owned by high-end art dealer Larry Fleischman.

"Did you buy anything at the auction last night?" he asked me. I told him what I'd bought.

"You ignoramuses from the Midwest. You come to New York, and you don't know anything about anything, and you don't talk to an expert."

What a way to do business. I call it "Technique Number 213"—salespeople are as rude as can be, and then if you don't walk out, they think they've established trust. They figure you'll assume that they're always going to be honest, because why would they say something so rude to you if it wasn't honest?

"What are you interested in?" he asked.

"Will you show me your three best things?" I asked, which is what I always ask dealers.

He pulled out three worthless paintings, and I politely walked out. It was a sucker test: he showed me bad paintings at high prices to see whether I really was an ignoramus. Unfortunately for him, I wasn't, and I never bought anything from him. Normally, it didn't matter to me where I bought a piece—whether it was Christie's, Sotheby's, or a relatively unknown dealer. I bought from whoever had the pieces I wanted. However, I could be pushed only so far. Larry was so insulting that I just stopped going to see what he had. Apparently, I wasn't the only one who had that experience: a collector friend of mine from Zurich turned apoplectic when I mentioned Larry's name at a dinner party.

After I came back from New York, I realized that I'd come to a fork in the road in my collecting. I now had five pictures and could have gone in two logical directions. I bought a Sheeler and a Davis to go with my Glackens and Burchfield, but I also bought a Bierstadt. Was I going early twentieth century or nineteenth century?

"Just think of the mistake I could have made had I gone with Homer, Sargent, Church, and Bierstadt!" I like to joke. Of course, that would have been a great collection, too. I could have taken both forks, but I felt I needed to discipline myself as a collector. My focus would lean toward early-twentieth-century American modernist art.

People have asked me whether Charles Buckley was my mentor. He wasn't. My mentor was my eye. I never took an art history class. I trained myself by looking at the art up close in museums, and I'm sure I'm one of the few collectors who can claim to have seen as many great works as I have. Many art history teachers, critics, and scholars rely on seeing great works in books, but that's not the same experience at all. You need to see a painting in person to really understand it.

For a long time, I didn't understand abstract art, but I never became cynical about it. I wanted to understand it, so I continued looking. Then, one day I had an epiphany—I call it my Saul-to-Paul conversion. I wanted so much to understand abstract art that I was intellectualizing it too much. It was like competing to be the best Buddhist in the world, completely contrary to the point. As I stood staring at a Picasso in a museum, I turned my brain off and just let the painting happen. It seemed to flow out, and all at once, I "got it." After such a long time of not really understanding him, Picasso became one of my favorite artists.

Although Charles Buckley was not my mentor per se, I would call him a guide. He introduced me to several honest and reputable art dealers, including Joan Washburn, Antoinette Kraushaar, and Virginia Zabriskie. He also gave me plenty of interesting advice. He suggested that in order to focus, I should build a collection of the best 12 American modernist paintings I could buy. Then, if I should find a thirteenth painting that was better than one I owned, I should sell that painting and buy the new one.

"Charles, I think that's a wonderful concept, but to me, that's like saying you can have 12 children, and when you have the thirteenth, you take little Bobby behind the barn and shoot him. I just don't think I can do it."

About a year later, I bought pictures 13, 14, and 15 on the same day and never looked back.

Due to luck, timing, and research, I managed to put together the best privately owned collection of American modernist paintings in existence. Only one other collection competes with mine, and ours will be the only two significant collections because of the dearth of great American modernists still in private ownership. I bought my first pictures in 1972, and although I've never stopped looking, there's very little to buy now. Each year, the market shrinks as the great works find homes in museums. Although I was not public about it, I had built my collection with the plan to leave it to a museum.

I have donated to museums all throughout my adult life, as well. I was only 39 when Charles Buckley invited me to become a trustee at the St. Louis Art Museum in 1973. I told him I was too young and that I'd love to do it someday when I had more experience.

"No, just come right in," he said. "You can just be quiet and listen for a couple of years."

I enjoyed being on the board and soon gained my footing. When the Egyptian mummy that originally drew me into the St. Louis Art Museum when I was a child was given back to its owner, Washington University, I bought another mummy for the museum. In 1989, I bought the mummy Amen-Nestawy-Nakht, a cleric at the temple of Karnak, and dedicated it to the children of St. Louis. I liked the idea of drawing more children into the museum. I called it a "kid catcher." I've continued to look for mummies for the Honolulu and Seattle Art Museums as well, but after periods of grave looting and illegal smuggling, the Egyptian Supreme Council of Antiquities created stringent laws that prohibit mummies from being sent out of Egypt.

When my daughter, Christiane, turned 16, I gave my Dutch paintings to her. Christiane had taken a significant interest in art and would go on to Sotheby's Institute of Art's postgraduate program and work in Sotheby's Department of Trusts, Estates, and Appraisals.

Aside from that, I had willed the majority of my pictures to the St. Louis Art Museum. It's a good thing I never told the museum, since neither the collection nor I would wind up in St. Louis.

---- *Chapter Ten* ----

GEORGIA
O'KEEFFE

T he next auction I attended was the estate of the great Edith Gregor Halpert, who owned Downtown Gallery. She had originally named it Our Gallery in 1926, and after Alfred Stieglitz died, she became the primary American modernist dealer. Sotheby Parke-Bernet sold her collection on March 14, 1973. On reflection, I should have bought the top 20 pictures she had, because another American modernist auction of that scope will never occur again. I still have two copies of the auction catalog in my office and recently paid $1,500,000 for a picture that sold for $35,000 at that auction. Same picture but with the added value of hindsight.

On that day, however, I bid on a great Marin watercolor that was estimated at $10,000 to $15,000; I bid to $46,000 and then stopped. It went for $47,500 to John D. Rockefeller, who was putting together a solid collection. I've often thought I cost him about $25,000 by bidding it up. That auction record stood until about 10 years ago.

I bought a Georgia O'Keeffe painting for $47,000 that is worth $8 to $10 million in today's world, so I'd say I did pretty well for myself. Charles Buckley was with me at that auction, and when it ended, he said, "Would you have time to meet Lloyd Goodrich?"

Lloyd had been the curator and director of the Whitney Museum of Art and had done the O'Keeffe retrospective in 1970 with Doris Bry. He was the foremost authority on Georgia O'Keeffe, and he'd written a great deal of the books I'd read on American art. Asking whether I had time to meet him was like asking whether I could fit in a meeting with the president of the United States.

"Young man, in my opinion, you've bought O'Keeffe's greatest picture," he said. He was referring to *Black, White and Blue*, a sharp abstract that she painted in 1930 in New Mexico. "You might wonder why it wasn't in my retrospective." He went on to explain that, due to a falling-out, Georgia and her agent and confidante, Doris Bry, didn't want to ask Edith Halpert to borrow the picture. Edith had been Georgia's exclusive dealer, but Georgia was known for having an abrasive personality. Eventually, she had fallings-out with just about everyone.

I knew I'd bought a great picture, but to hear Lloyd proclaim it her best was a thrill. I think the reason I understood Georgia's work was that I came to American artists with European eyes; Europeans understood this type of art long before Americans did. We still had a cultural inferiority complex that told us that all great works of art came from Europe. American art didn't blossom until after World War II with artists such as Pollock, de Kooning, Kline, and Rothko. Georgia's work showed no European influence; it didn't feel derivative of anything. It was purely American and undeniably Georgia.

Georgia's style and subject matter changed through the years. Her flowers and bones were both wonderful, but, in my opinion, the abstractions were her real contribution to art. At the auction, her 1952 painting of two flowers sold for $127,000, a record-breaking figure for an O'Keeffe, and yet I wouldn't own that picture. I found it flabby. I'd love a 1930 flower or bone picture, but I wouldn't want a picture from when her career was in its decline.

It's not that Georgia's work was ever bad—it's just that her later work is nothing compared to her earlier work. Same with Picasso: dealers can sell his late pictures for $10 to $20 million, even though they're terrible compared to what he used to do, just because he's Picasso. At any price, I wouldn't want a late Picasso, though I'd love to own a great one.

Buying work by Georgia violated my "no living artists" rule, though her career was long over by that time. She had suffered a nervous breakdown in 1932 when she fell far behind schedule painting a mural for Radio City Music Hall. Stieglitz had strongly opposed the project, construction had delayed the start, and Georgia ended up walking off and quitting. It was her first public failure and revealed for the first time her self-doubt and concerns about her abilities. It also coincided with her discovery that her husband was having an obvious affair with a gallery volunteer in her twenties named Dorothy Norman. She knew he was interested in Dorothy before that but thought it was just an infatuation. Now Stieglitz was being cruel to Georgia and showing up to public events with his young mistress.

Within just a few days after quitting the Radio City commission, Georgia experienced a wide range of physical and emotional problems that lasted for several months—shortness of breath, unexplained crying spells, pain, a weakened immune system, and so on. She was treated at Doctors Hospital in New York for psychoneurosis and then traveled and recuperated for the next year, during which time she didn't produce any paintings. Afterward, her art was never the same. She painted again, but things were missing—at one point, she could paint a circle that seemed to go on forever, and she lost that ability after her breakdown. One thing about a breakdown like that: you learn how *not* to have another one. Unfortunately, the side effect was less intense art.

Georgia was a very devoted artist, though. She awoke before dawn some days to go outside and paint the sunrise. Other days, she walked around in search of the perfect rocks or bones to paint— she was always collecting things to study. Her relationship with art was more stable than her relationship with people. Even after she married Stieglitz, she traveled from New York to New Mexico for long stretches each summer because she felt she had to be alone to do her artwork. Once he died, she moved to Abiquiu permanently and primarily lived life as a loner, save for her relationship with Doris Bry.

"Who bought that great picture?" Georgia asked Doris after the Halpert auction. Georgia famously hated selling her paintings and would refuse to sell to people she didn't approve of—which was at the heart of her falling-out with Edith Halpert. Georgia always maintained that she painted for herself, not for the market.

"Barney Ebsworth, a collector. I know him—he's a good guy," Doris told her. We had met through Charles Buckley.

Soon thereafter, my phone rang, and it was Doris.

"Georgia would like you to come down to Abiquiu and meet her," she said.

"Well, I don't know whether I can do that," I replied. I ended up turning her down for two reasons: one was that I was genuinely very busy and the other was that I knew Georgia was private and I was private.

I understood that it was an honor to receive an invitation from Georgia, who often had uninvited guests show up at her door. One time, a pushy New Yorker rang the bell and said, "I'm here to see O'Keeffe." Georgia said, "Well, there's O'Keeffe's front, there's O'Keefe's side, there's O'Keeffe's rear end. You've seen O'Keeffe." Then she slammed the door.

Doris called with another invitation the next year, and again I turned her down. A few months later came another invitation—I think she was baffled that I kept saying no when everyone else was clamoring to meet her—and I thought about it overnight.

One day I'm going to read in the New York Times *obituaries that she died,* I thought. It was 1974, and Georgia was 87 years old by then. *This may be my last opportunity.*

I called Doris and said, "I'd like to take up the invitation."

Doris flew from New York to meet me there. When I arrived at Georgia's door, the first thing that struck me was her commanding presence. She wore all black, as was her usual, and although she was not a large woman, she seemed so.

I've met presidents and all kinds of celebrities, and I've never felt this intimidated, I thought.

Luckily, an icebreaker presented itself: the silver pin she wore. I'd seen it in several photos and never knew what it was. Up close, I realized that it said "OK," short for "O'Keeffe." It was her mark—the same one she used when she signed the pictures she liked best. She'd sign her favorites "OK" with a little Star of David around it. My major O'Keeffes have this designation.

"That must be your favorite pin," I said. "I've seen it in photos and always thought it was a Navajo pin, but now I see it's your initials."

"Yes," she said. "It was given to me by Alexander Calder. But this isn't the one he did for me. He made it in bronze, but it didn't match my hair. When I went around the world for the first time, the silversmiths in India were so good that I asked them to make it for me in silver."

Aha, I thought. *This is a regular woman. A woman who wants her jewelry to match her hair.*

"I didn't know that was your initials!" Doris said.

"You've been looking at it for 20 years and never noticed that?"

She laughed, and the ice was broken. Although everyone around her called her "Miss O'Keeffe," I felt comfortable calling

BOX—IV.

her Georgia, and she never objected. She and I quickly became friends after that trip, and I went to visit her in New Mexico many times. She never came to me; I always went to her. I think she knew how much I appreciated her and that I wasn't going to exploit her in any way. On about my fourth trip to see her, we were sitting out at Ghost's Ranch, the site of the other home she owned, and I said, "Would you mind if I take pictures of you?"

"Well, I'd just as soon you didn't, but if you want to, go ahead."

"I won't, then."

And that was that. The fact that she was so straightforward with me meant that I could be straightforward with her, too. Georgia didn't like to explain her pictures, so it was unusual for her to comment on them. However, she gave me a cryptic clue about the painting I owned, *Black, White and Blue*: "This was a message to a friend—if he saw it, he didn't know it was to him and wouldn't have known what it said. And neither do I."

"Georgia," I said, "I read T. S. Eliot in college. I didn't know what in the world he was talking about, and I don't know what you're talking about." Still, I thought it was a brilliant nonanswer. She was very good at remaining mysterious.

If I had to identify when Georgia was at her strongest in life, it was the year she painted that picture, 1930. She'd spent her life traveling and had just found her place in her beloved New Mexico, the place where she'd live the rest of her life.

A year after I bought my first O'Keeffe, Doris called to tell me that Georgia had decided to sell her other great abstract painting from her personal collection, *Music—Pink and Blue No. 1*, which she'd painted in 1919. She wanted it to hang next to her other great abstract: the one I owned. I bought it. Barbara Haskell, the great Whitney curator of American Art, said I now owned her best masculine abstract painting and her best feminine abstract painting.

Doris lived on the fourth floor of the Pulitzer Mansion on East 73rd, and one of my close friends, Joe Pulitzer, was the grandson of Joseph Pulitzer. Charles Buckley said, "Call Joe when you get home. Have him come see the picture and tell him you found it in his grandfather's attic."

Over time, I bought three more of Georgia's pieces. The next was an unusual situation—Doris had taken on a side project wherein she made a limited-edition booklet of 20 of Georgia's drawings. Later, she made another version in large format, producing only 100 copies. "Would you like one?" she asked me that summer.

"I definitely want one. Send it to me and I'll look at it on a cold, rainy winter night in St. Louis with the fire going."

That's exactly what I did. In November, I pulled out the drawing book for the first time, and what struck me was a gorgeous portrait of a black man: the charcoal drawing *Beauford Delaney* from the early 1940s. It reminded me of a drawing she had done in Bermuda of a banana flower in the 1930s; the way the man was situated on the page was just like the way she had placed the banana flower.

I called over my girlfriend, Trish. "Look at this," I said. "Look at this unbelievable portrait she's drawn."

It made me wonder why she didn't draw more portraits. Georgia had very rarely drawn people, but she made five portraits of Beauford, a kind-hearted artist who suffered from mental illness. She said he was "a very special person—impossible to define."

Just as I was discussing the drawing with Trish, the phone rang, and it was Doris Bry. Doris hadn't called me in months.

"Remember that book you sent me last summer?" I asked her. "I just discovered *Beauford Delaney*, and I've never seen anything like it. It's absolutely wonderful. If you'd called two minutes earlier, I wouldn't have had this conversation with you. I see that the Met and the Modern own most of the pictures in this book. Whom does this one belong to?"

"It belongs to Georgia, and it's hanging in front of me this very minute."

I swallowed. "Would it be for sale?"

"It would be for you."

I bought it on the spot. It was the first picture I ever bought by ESP.

Dinner at Georgia's house was always spare: a small piece of organic beef and organic peas or string beans that she grew on her property, with a little glass of Bordeaux wine. Plain but very good. She lived healthfully.

After dinner, we'd retire to the living room with Juan Hamilton, a man 58 years her junior who had shown up on her doorstep at Ghost Ranch looking for work in 1973. In the ensuing time, he had become her live-in companion and had significant influence over her life and her art. I always hoped that he wouldn't join us in the living room, because I was there for her. I liked Juan well enough, but he was an interloper as far as I was concerned, and he probably thought the same of me.

Georgia and I often talked about Stieglitz and the artists who surrounded them at the time: John Marin, Arthur Dove, Charles Demuth. It was good for her; she enjoyed reminiscing and telling stories, and I enjoyed hearing them.

One of her funniest tales was about a time in 1925 when she was hanging a Marsden Hartley retrospective at the Intimate Gallery. She was standing on a stepladder when Hartley walked by.

"Marsden, would you hand me that hammer?" she asked.

He looked at her incredulously and said, "But I'm the artist."

There Georgia was hanging his show, and he wouldn't even hand her a hammer.

We'd get into long talks many nights where the hours would drift past. On one such night, she turned to me and asked, "Did you really like the color of the walls at 291?"

"Georgia, Alfred closed 291 sixteen years before I was born."

It was fun knowing that she could get so lost in our talks that she'd forget I wasn't around in the 1920s. Juan would interject his thoughts in the conversation, once giving a 45-minute monologue about Georgia's work. She had painted her last oil picture unassisted at age 84 in 1972, shortly after her eyesight began failing. Since then, she had continued painting with assistance, looking through binoculars and directing her helpers.

Juan was also teaching her how to create pottery. Colors had become gray and muted to her, and she was likely legally blind.

That fact was apparently of no consequence to Juan, who built to a crescendo in his monologue thusly: "Georgia did great work in the teens and better work in the '20s and '30s. Then she got better again in the '40s, even better in the '50s and '60s, and now in the '70s, she's doing her best work! You agree with that, don't you, Barney?"

I looked at him, and with Georgia sitting right opposite me, I said, "Juan, that is pure, unmitigated bullshit." I found it no coincidence that he claimed she was doing her best work in the '70s, when he showed up. I was a bit embarrassed to say what I needed to say in front of her, but I couldn't hold it in. "She burst on the scene in a wonderful way and did fabulous work in 1918 and 1919. In the '20s she got better and better, and I think 1930 was probably her best year. And then in '32, she had her collapse. After '32, she never did a 100 percent cutting-edge picture again. In fact, the best picture she did after 1932 is the one right behind you." I pointed to the 1944 oil painting *Black Place III*.

Juan blew his top.

"You dumb jerk! You don't know what you're talking about!" he said, steam wafting from his ears.

"Juan, you're full of it."

"Georgia, tell Barney he doesn't know what he's talking about."

She said, "Barney knows what he's talking about."

That was the end of the conversation.

The art world at the time was buzzing with the titillating gossip that Juan and Georgia were having a love affair, but I wouldn't even entertain that idea. Some infatuation may have existed on Georgia's part because he was a man nearly 60 years her junior, good-looking, and intelligent, and I'm sure Juan was likewise infatuated with her talent and fame, but a romance? No. Juan liked to fan the rumors, though.

People always ask me what Georgia was like, because so few people really knew her. Myriad books were written about Georgia, and few of them reflect the woman I knew. She was very human but like a hermit. She didn't waste words; everything was crisp and sharp, to the point. She spoke like she painted. Always, she was listening to and observing nature.

"I can hear a dog barking in the distance," she'd say. "That's so poetic."

People were only peripherally important. She was diabolical in the way she sabotaged her friendships. She just left men, but women—women she tore to shreds. She liked being in control of all her relationships and wrote people off flatly when they crossed her in even minor ways. Once Juan had a foothold in her life, she ended many of her long-standing business and personal relationships—agent Doris Bry and cook Jerrie Newsom were among the casualties. She gave Juan the power to screen her calls and her mail and to fire people who worked for her. He was as diabolical as she was, but I was not on the chopping block because Juan realized I had no ulterior motives and could be useful.

Early in our friendship, I could see that trouble was brewing between Doris and Juan. Anyone with the right sensibilities could see that Doris was on her way out in Georgia's life, and that wasn't going to end well. After all, Doris had a contract to be Georgia's exclusive agent, and now Juan was honing in on her territory.

Sure enough, I was right, and I started getting calls from both of them about the injustices of the other. A lawsuit was clearly coming. I begged them both not to sue each other.

"Once you call lawyers in, you've hired killers on each side, and they're each going to try to 'win' and keep the meter running," I said. "Don't let it get to that." My belief was that you don't ever want to be on that road unless there's no other possible way out.

It was too deep-seated, though, and they couldn't listen to me, at least at first. Both sides hired expensive lawyers. Doris filed a claim because she believed she had a lifetime agreement to sell the pictures at a 25 percent commission, whereas Georgia complained that she didn't want to sell pictures to just anybody and wanted her agent to place them with people who were hand selected as good caretakers. The paperwork said that the basis for the lawsuit was breach of agency contract, but what it really came down to was alienation of affection, divorce, and removal from the will.

A year later, Georgia called me on a Saturday morning and said, "You're the only one we trust and whom we think Doris would trust, too. Will you mediate the lawsuit?"

"I'm not a lawyer, and I've never mediated a lawsuit," I said, but that didn't matter to her. After some thought, I realized that mediation was really about fair play and common sense. Having run several companies with hundreds of employees, I had effectually been mediating all the time.

I agreed to do it. Doris was relieved to hear my voice; both sides had already spent more than a million dollars on legal bills, and I don't think she had much more left to her name. For the next four months, I heard from both of them regularly, but Doris was the nocturnal one who'd call at 1:00 in the morning and wake Trish.

"Can I talk to Barney?" she'd say, skipping right past the "Hello" and "How are you?" She'd talk to me for an hour about all of it—the financial issues and the emotional issues driving the lawsuit. Of course, I couldn't solve their emotional issues; that was something they'd have to come to grips with themselves, but I tried hard to be there for both of them and to find common ground where they could settle. Before long, I had to start medication for an upset stomach, but I hoped I was making progress with them.

It was a bit like Michelangelo's process of chipping away at a block of stone little by little and hoping there was a statue in there somewhere. After four months of negotiations, I could see the compromise—all I had to do was get each of them to give two inches more and we'd be there. That's the point when I had to take both of them by the hand and say, "Here's the deal. Now, you can agree to this or you can lose me and go back to your lawyers."

By that time, we had all invested a lot of time and effort, and they agreed to the terms. We had a financial agreement, and everyone was pleased with me. They all wanted to pay me something, but I said, "I didn't do it for money, and you can't afford me, anyway."

Juan said, "I want to give you one of my sculptures," and I said, "OK, I can accept that."

So the next time I came to the house, he told me to pick whichever one I wanted. There must have been 50 sculptures.

I picked one, and Georgia said, "You can't give Barney that one. That's mine!" Of all the pieces, I had picked Georgia's. He made me a similar sculpture instead.

Doris offered me several Stieglitz photographs, but I didn't feel right accepting—they were too valuable.

"What if I give them to the St. Louis Art Museum in your honor?"

"I think that's lovely," I said. The museum received the photographs as a gift.

Georgia asked me what she could do. It would be a couple of years before I came up with an answer.

Like me, Georgia didn't much like the telephone. When we talked by phone, it was just to set up an appointment to meet or usually when she wanted something. But one day in 1981, I called with an unusual request for her.

I had been living with Trish for several years, and we had decided to get married. We agreed on a small wedding but were presented with a dilemma once the time came to make a guest list. If we were going to invite this one, we had to invite that one, and so on. It went from a list of 10 to 25 to 100 to 200 in short order. There was no cutoff, and it wasn't what either of us wanted.

"We need to go somewhere to get married where nobody's invited," I told Trish. That's when I had the perfect idea.

"Georgia, do you owe me a favor?" I asked over the phone.

"Barney, whatever you want."

"Can we come down to Abiquiu and get married at your house? That way we can tell people that nobody's invited—plus, you're the only person I know who could be the maid of honor *and* the best man."

She got a kick out of that and said yes. We ended up in Georgia's living room while we waited for the county judge to arrive. Most likely, he agreed to marry us purely to catch an inside glimpse of Georgia's house. So few people from the community had seen it. It was originally an adobe ranch house, and the place was much like she was: austere, uncluttered, with very little decoration. It had plenty of windows out of which to look and walls on which to hang her pictures.

The fireworks started as soon as the judge arrived, though. He wore his black polyester judicial robe, and Georgia greeted him at the door in her all-black dress.

"I thought I was going to be the only one wearing a black dress today," she said.

I don't think he was amused.

"Who are the witnesses?" he asked.

"Pieta and I are the witnesses," she said. Pieta Lopez was her secretary.

"Oh, no, I need a male and a female witness."

"I don't think I made myself clear. Pieta and I are the witnesses."

"No, that's not allowed."

Georgia was wonderful to be with. Once she made up her mind about something, it was going to be that way or no way.

The Lopez family all worked for Georgia; Pieta was the secretary, her mother was the cook, her grandfather was the head gardener, and two of her brothers also tended the gardens. I looked out the window.

"Isn't that Maggie out there? Would you ask him to step in here?" Maggie was one of Pieta's brothers, whose name wound up in one of Georgia's paintings: *A Sunflower from Maggie.*

Maggie approached, and I asked, "What are you doing for the next half hour?"

"Whatever you want. What can I do for you, Mr. Ebsworth?"

"You're my best man."

Throughout the ceremony, Georgia kept squeezing Trish's hand and saying things like, "I don't believe in marriage. I'm just doing this for Barney."

She had attended one wedding in her life: her own. The only two guests present were John Martin and Stieglitz's niece Georgia Engelhardt. The foursome drove across the Hudson River Bridge to New Jersey in 1924 and saw a justice of the peace. So after my wedding, I liked to remind Georgia, "You've been to only two weddings—yours and mine!"

She was a funny woman, and when she told a joke, you'd catch a rare peek at her softer side: she had almost a little-girlish giggle. Few writers or filmmakers ever got it right, but a woman named Perry Miller Adato finally captured Georgia's spirit in a 1977 documentary.

In it, Georgia describes her first visit to New Mexico with her sister in 1917: "When I got to New Mexico, that was mine. As soon as I saw it, that was my country. I'd never seen anything like it before, but it fitted to me exactly. It's something that's in the air;

it's different. The sky is different; the wind is different. I shouldn't say too much about it because other people may be interested, and I don't want them interested."

Outsiders rarely made it past Georgia's gatekeeping scrutiny. Juan managed to get his wife in under the radar: he married a very nice woman named Anna Marie, and Georgia was gracious about it. Shortly thereafter, Juan called me to say that he and his wife were going to have a baby.

"Yes," I said. "You're going to have a boy, and he's going to be born on July 14."

Don't ask me. I don't know how I knew, but the truth is that I've had many inexplicable thoughts like this that came true over the course of my life. Sometimes I know facts about someone's past, and sometimes I know about things yet to come—and the best I can explain it is that I'm guessing. How I guess correctly is a mystery, but sure enough, their son was born on July 14, my birthday.

The next year, he said they were going to have another baby.

"Yes, another son, and he's going to be born on November 22, my daughter's birthday."

I was right again. I've never met the children, but I hope to someday.

In her final couple of years, Georgia moved in with Juan and his family in a big estate in Santa Fe. She was infirm by then and needed to be closer to a hospital. I didn't see her again.

Some time later, I visited Abiquiu with a good friend, Liz Glassman, president of the Georgia O'Keeffe Foundation.

"My friend got married here in O'Keeffe's house," she told the excellent guide.

"You've been inside? You knew Georgia?" he asked.

When I said I had, he turned the tour over to me. He was one of the best guides I'd ever known, but his knowledge was through reading, whereas mine was firsthand. I loved the experience of telling the people about Georgia and Abiquiu. Then and now, I've always tried to be circumspect about the most personal details of her life. I figure that she put her trust in me for a reason.

Georgia was warm, but first one had to get through so much outer crust. Being with her was like being with a Buddhist monk—she was so self-contained that when you got a piece of her, you were really getting something. It wasn't watered down.

She changed my perception about collecting works only by dead artists; as I grew older, I realized that knowing the creators of art had value, too. Now I wish I had met all of the artists whose works I've collected. I ended up meeting many celebrated artists through the years, but Georgia will always be special to me. I miss her.

Chapter Eleven

THE
EXPERIENCE

I never liked being in the glare of the media, particularly after a few bad experiences with journalists, so I've lived my life in relative anonymity. Still, at times I granted interviews because it was for a greater good: because it served to promote my business interests, my art collection, or my philanthropic interests, which were often intertwined.

During one such interview with Steve Wiecking, a writer for *Seattle Metropolitan* magazine, he asked, "If you had the choice between having the pictures or having the experience, which would you take?"

"Well, that's easy," I responded. "It'd be the experience—the experience of learning what a picture is. You have to *like* a picture."

It's what I advise any new art lovers who ask me about collecting. Particularly if you're buying contemporary art, you have to go into it without concern about the appreciation value: more than 99 percent of contemporary art won't ever be worth more than what you paid for it, no matter how an art dealer tries to hype it. Dealers don't have masterworks to sell; they're selling whatever they can as soon as the paint dries. So the question then becomes one of taste: which pictures do you want to live with? Which ones come alive for you? There's no point in buying a picture if you don't really like it.

It may sound disingenuous because my collection has significantly increased in value, but I didn't buy artwork as investments. I bought the pieces because I had done a lot of looking and decided these were great pictures and I wanted to live with them.

I have been fortunate enough to be able to afford to own great works, but had I not been wealthy, I still would have had the opportunity to know great art. Museums and libraries are available to everyone, and I have found great pleasure and satisfaction in learning about art. Owning the pictures doesn't make a person a scholar. So many MFAs and PhDs who lecture about art have learned about it by looking at slides, so if you've seen the real objects, you're already a step ahead. With this in mind, my philanthropy has focused on art.

Although I collected with the plan to donate to a museum, I liked that I didn't have to get approval from a museum board when I bought. I spent my own money, so I get to live with the pictures in my lifetime. Over time, my limits kept increasing.

I bought Marsden Hartley's painting *Berlin 49* for $125,000, the most I'd spent on a picture at that time. It was from his best period. Then in 1973, I went to visit a dealer, Bill Zierler, who'd sold me a terrific Edward Hopper watercolor titled *Cottages at*

North Truro, Massachusetts, and this time, he had a magnificent oil painting from 1929, *Chop Suey.* It depicted two women sitting in a Chinese restaurant—a good way to get cheap but tasty food during the Depression. It looked like a movie scene, as many of Hopper's paintings do. I found it stunning, but the dealer wanted $200,000. I just didn't think I should spend that much on a picture, and I never negotiate. If a dealer sees that you're a haggler, he or she just adds 10 percent to the asking price and you wind up at the same spot anyway.

"Think about it," Bill said before I left that day.

When I didn't call back right away, he called me. "Barney, don't you want to buy this picture?"

"Bill, I think it's great, and I think it's a fair price. There's no problem. It's just that I'm not prepared to spend that much money."

"Let me call the owners and see whether they'll drop the price."

He called back half an hour later with the news that they'd be willing to take 10 percent less: $180,000.

"That's very fair, but I'm still not ready to spend that much on a picture."

I really did love it, though, and I started thinking through ways to make it work. "Wait a minute," I said. "I bought that Hopper watercolor from you last year for $65,000. If I send it back to you and you give me back my money, then that brings the price down to $115,000. I'm willing to spend $115,000."

It was really just some mental gymnastics to get myself to jump over the fence I'd created for myself.

"Barney, I can't do that. I don't own the picture—it's on consignment, and I can't afford to make that deal."

So I got creative: "I'll give you an interest-free loan for the $65,000, and you can take a year to pay me."

"Done," he said. "Send me a letter, and the transaction will be completed."

Three days later, I received a special-delivery letter confirming the deal. I carefully considered the letter, looked at my watercolor, and sent Bill a check for $180,000. I couldn't part with it, and I had released myself from the monetary constraints I'd put on myself. Now that I'd broken through that barrier, I had opened myself up to spend more than $180,000 on a picture. I just kept inching my way up.

Chop Suey appeared on the cover of the catalog for the first show of my collection, and it has appeared in more than 30 exhibitions.

That's how close I came to passing up the greatest picture in my collection.

I was offered $60 million for it in the late 1990s but turned it down. No great Hoppers are left on the market, and mine has become quite precious to me. About 20 years ago, I bought another terrific Hopper that I love almost as much, *The French Six-Day Bicycle Rider*, inspired by Hopper's many visits to watch the indoor bicycle races at Madison Square Garden. *The French Six-Day Bicycle Rider* is among the paintings I'm leaving to my daughter, because when she's an old woman, she'll likely be the only person left to own an Edward Hopper oil painting. The rest will all be in museums.

Chop Suey became a good bargaining chip, too. The Seattle Art Museum wanted to borrow another of Hopper's great pieces, *Automat*, from the Des Moines Art Center but hadn't received an acceptance.

"Tell them I'll loan them *Chop Suey* for three months next winter if they let us borrow *Automat*." It worked.

The art world led me to meet many interesting people. One of my favorites is Steve Martin, who has a deep interest in American modernism as well. I was in Steve's New York apartment before I ever met him because a friend of mine in St. Louis was considering buying a nineteenth-century American picture that Steve owned. My friend couldn't make it to New York to see the picture, so he asked me to go to put my stamp of approval on it. Along with the dealer, I went to the Carlyle Hotel in Manhattan, where Steve had an apartment.

Before leaving, I asked the dealer, "Would you mind if I go to the bathroom and get a glass of water?"

"Sure, go ahead."

I did so and then asked, "Do you know why I did that?"

"Because you were thirsty?"

"No. I want to be able to say I had a drink in Steve Martin's apartment."

A couple of years later we were introduced to each other, and he invited me over. He wasn't like his on-screen persona when we were together. I doubt his fans realize how intellectual he is—very serious, very smart, understated, and very kind. We met again many times through our art connections and developed a friendship.

We're similar souls, passionate about art. Like me, he cares about understanding the pictures, not just amassing a collection of "name" artists.

Mostly, we talked about art. The first time I visited, he was amazed that I was able to identify the artist of every piece in his home. His collection included many relatively unknown artists.

"Nobody has ever been able to name every artist before," he said.

"You're not the only wild and crazy guy in this house now," I said.

I attended a small dinner party thrown by Ronnie Greenberg where Andy Warhol was the guest of honor. Just five or six of us were there, and we spent the whole evening together. He never spoke one word. That was apparently his norm; no one expected him to talk. I knew he was notoriously quiet, but I was still taken by surprise that he literally didn't say one word. I didn't feel as though it was an act; it's just the way he was.

Similarly, I spent 12 hours with Ed Sullivan at the Carlton Hotel in Cannes, because we had a mutual friend, and Ed spoke one sentence the whole time. We spent time on the beach and had lunch and dinner together, and at about 10:00, he said, "I'm tired; I'm going to go to bed." That was all. His wife was the talker. At least Ed was a good listener. He was less placid than

Andy Warhol was—he seemed interested in the conversation, just disinclined to talk.

My first meeting with Dan Terra was an amusing one; although we'd never met in person, he invited me to the opening of his museum in Chicago in 1980. At the museum that day, I stood with Trish in front of Arthur Dove's pastel *A Walk: Poplars*, which was under glass. I was telling her about the picture when I felt a tap on my shoulder. There was Dan Terra, smiling and saying, "I see you're looking at *A Walk: Poplars*. That's Arthur Dove's; he painted it in 1919." Everything he said was right there on the label.

"Yes, I know," I said. "In fact, it was sold at the famous Edith Halpert sale on March 14, 1973, for $19,000. Joe Pulitzer almost bought it for $45,000, but my friend Rolf Weinberg bought it and sold it to you, along with a Marsden Hartley 1914 painting."

There was a short pause.

"Do you have a card?"

I handed him my business card. As he walked away, I elbowed Trish and laughed. "Right now, he's staring at my card thinking, 'Who in the world is that guy?'"

The party that night was at the Drake Hotel's grand ballroom, and it was unlike any museum opening gala I've been to. Dan was a major fundraiser for President Reagan, and in turn, he became the first and only U.S. Ambassador of Art. At the party, everyone lined up to have a photo taken with the ambassador and his wife, but afterward, no one got copies. I'm not sure whether the camera had no film or whether no one really knew who all the people were so they couldn't match us up to send the photos.

Then the lights dimmed, and a big band began to play *Yankee Doodle Dandy*. I was seated with two sophisticated art dealers from New York, one of whom didn't look amused. But he was horrified by what happened next: Dan Terra, dressed as Uncle Sam, came tap dancing across the stage singing "I'm a Yankee Doodle Dandy!"

I thought it was terrific, one of the most memorable moments of my life. My friend Stuart, however, had his eyes on the ceiling.

"What's wrong, Stuart?" I asked.

"You wouldn't do something like this, Barney."

"I would if I had the talent."

Dan was a very good entertainer, extroverted and fun. He sure knew how to shake things up in the sometimes-uptight art world.

The only kind of snobbery I can stand is intellectual snobbery. I enjoy being around scholars and collectors who have taken their time to learn about art for reasons aside from bragging rights. I've been to many art fairs and never had the desire to go back to any of them because I don't enjoy the cocktail party aspect of it. It feels like a social status contest rather than a day to appreciate fine art. It becomes about being seen, hobnobbing with the media, and outspending your archenemy.

Auctions, likewise, have changed over the years. When I began collecting, the cast of characters was familiar—you could identify all the major collectors and dealers. Generally, no members of the press were present, you didn't need a ticket, and you could sit where you wanted without causing a stir. I called it a "gentlemen's auction."

Attending my first modern art auction was a shocking experience. A few months before my first exhibition, I had decided that once the show was over, I would expand my collection to the last part of the twentieth century. The first picture I wanted to buy was the largest picture: James Rosenquist's *F-111*. It was 86 feet wide and 10 feet high, filling all four walls of a room. I didn't really know what I was going to do with it, but thought I might build a room onto my house with black marble flooring and a great stereo system to play Vietnam-era music.

It was like the Academy Awards—anyone who wasn't a player couldn't get a ticket, and it was standing room only, with two or three peripheral rooms participating via TV screens. At auctions, my favorite seat was the aisle of the sixth row, center section. Eli Broad liked the fifth-row aisle, so I was often behind him. But this time, they seated me in the first row, right under the auctioneer's nose. I believe they knew what I was there to buy and wanted to draw attention to it.

The only thing I didn't know about the picture I wanted was its condition. It had been in a show at the Whitney Museum six months prior, so I went to see my friend Patterson Sims, who was its chief curator at the time.

"Can you tell me about the condition of *F-111*?" I asked him. I watched his face drop and "Oh, gosh. You're going to try to buy it for the Whitney."

"Well, Tom Armstrong, the director, would like to buy it."

This was the time when the power had just shifted from the museums to private collectors. It used to be that you'd worry when a museum wanted to bid against you, but now I knew that I could outbid any museum.

The estimate was about $1 million. My auction technique was to wait until the end to bid. You just have to make one bid: the winning one. I knocked out Tom at $1.25 million, but another bidder had the same "wait until the end" technique as I did, and the two of us ran the price up to $2 million in about 12 seconds. That was my limit. I go into auctions with a set figure in my mind of how high I'm willing to go, and I've violated that only three or four times and never by much.

The frenzied end of the auction erupted in such a flash that it was hard to tell who had won, but Jeffrey Deitch had made the winning bid. The room burst into applause since the previous record had been $175,000.

Out of nowhere, a female "paratrooper" descended on me—or, then again, maybe she was just a reporter.

"What's your name?"

My adrenaline was still racing from the bidding. I looked at her.

"Where are you from?"

I said nothing.

"Are you a collector or a professional? I'm Rita Reif from the *New York Times*."

I pointed my finger and said, "I don't wish to speak to you. Leave."

She did. A few moments later, the woman sitting behind me said, "Congratulations, Sir. You've bought a great picture. Where are you going to put it?"

"Well, thank you," I said, "but, actually, I was the underbidder, and I have not the foggiest idea where I was going to put it. If you know where you're going to put it, you're not a great collector."

The buyer didn't know where to put it, either. It sat in storage for about 15 years until he sold it to MOMA. That museum put the piece all together on one wall rather than letting it fill all four walls of a room, which I thought was a poor choice the first time I saw it. Now it's grown on me a bit, and I can accept that it works that way, too.

My wife pointed out the *New York Times* article the day after the auction that noted how significantly the painting had broken the world record for a Rosenquist—of course, it was by far his best work. It also included the dimensions of the painting.

"Darn," I said. "If I had just thought about it in terms of price per square inch, I would have realized it was a bargain and I could have bid higher!"

A month later, the Joseph Stella masterpiece *Tree of My Life* came up for auction, and it again blew past the estimate of $800,000–$900,000. When it hit the $2 million mark, I didn't have the same psychological hurdle holding me back as my, as it turned out, two competitors did. I bid $2,000,000, and they dropped out.

My friend Alice Walton built a beautiful museum called Crystal Bridges in Bentonville, Arkansas, using her own money. It has no charge for admission, and she has a notable collection of American art. Friends of mine on the East Coast said, "What a waste. It's in the Ozark Mountains."

"What do you mean? In the area between St. Louis and Dallas and Kansas City, there were no great museums. She's built an institution in an area that needed it."

That's an important legacy that resonates with me, and it's why I've been so committed to lending out my works and giving them to museums.

My collection's first exhibition was in St. Louis, opening on November 20, 1987. It felt like time; the director had asked me whether the museum could exhibit my collection, and I felt it was complete enough to form a meaningful stand-alone show of American modernism. The exhibit was titled *The Ebsworth Collection: American Modernism, 1911–1947*. Only after the show did I begin collecting later pieces.

I wanted to know what went into producing an art exhibition, and this one gave me all the insight I desired. Like many things in life, it looks simpler than it is—it took far longer and was more involved than I anticipated. I chose the three essayists for the catalog, and all three were museum directors or ex-directors: Charles Buckley, William Agee, and John Lane. I don't know of another exhibition where all of the essayists have been directors.

My friend Michael Shapiro, now the director of the High Museum of Art in Atlanta, was the curator of record. I chose the printer and the pictures and picked the venues (St. Louis Art Museum, Honolulu Academy of Arts, and Museum of Fine Arts in Boston). By the time of the exhibition, I was glad all the work was over and that I'd had the experience. In 2000, when the National Gallery asked to exhibit my collection—which now included works by later American artists such as Pollack, Johns, Rauschenberg, de Kooning, Warhol, and Kline—it was very different: all I had to do was sign off on the pictures I was willing to lend the museum and then stand back and let the machine do its work. My only specification was that the show also go to the Seattle Art Museum, since that was now where I lived. Aside from that, my lack of involvement didn't bother me at all; I'd satisfied my curiosity about running an exhibition with the previous show and had no desire to do it again.

I never lost my passion for the pictures, however. Every one of them means something to me. They're like old friends I get to visit whenever I want.

Chapter Twelve

RETIREMENT

In 1989, I began a 10-year plan to sell all the companies I owned before my sixty-fifth birthday on July 14, 1999. I didn't want to be responsible for so many employees after that time, and I wanted more time for my own pursuits. I was deeply enmeshed in the art world by then and knew I was not going to spend my retirement years in a deck chair.

I was glad to have given my company the name INTRAV, rather than something that bore my name, such as the Ebsworth Travel Company, because I didn't want my name associated with a company I no longer ran. INTRAV could be run by anyone.

Another thing that made it easier was a wise investment I'd made in a woman named Maxine Clark. I'd read a 1997 article in the *St. Louis Business Journal* about this enterprising woman and a business she was creating called Build-A-Bear Workshop. She had been president of Payless Shoes, selling 20 percent of all the shoes in America, but had gotten burned out. Payless was in

Topeka, Kansas, but Maxine's husband had a business in St. Louis, so they had both been traveling back and forth between the two until she quit and decided to start her own business in St. Louis. The idea for Build-A-Bear came to her while she was shopping with her friend's children and they were looking for a new Beanie Baby to buy. They couldn't find one they didn't already have, so the girl said, "We could make one." That set Maxine thinking about the possibilities of kids making their own stuffed animals.

Her prototype store wasn't open yet, but it sounded like a brilliant concept to me. I told the president of our venture capital company, "I like that gal. Get her business plan, and if you like it, I'll interview her."

Maxine was a dynamo with superb marketing sensibilities. She had a "Cub Advisory Board" composed of children—mainly preteen girls, since they were her customers. Why not talk to them about what you're doing?

"What a great way to enjoy being in business," I thought, and I agreed to become her partner, investing $4.2 million in the start-up. For once, someone else would do all the work, and I would have the easy role: all I did was make a smart investment, and I owned 40 percent of the business in return.

On opening day, there were lines out the door in our shop in the St. Louis Galleria mall. Build-A-Bear nearly doubled its sales projections in the first year and soon had stores in most major cities in the United States. The business was a terrific success. I felt sure that my investment would continue to pay off for years to come.

And so it was with a little sentimentality and a great deal of pride for what we'd accomplished that I retired in 1999. My businesses were my babies, and it was painful to part with them and entrust them with the next owners, although I knew it had to be done. I tried to pick people who would carry on the business well. A year later came the September 11 attacks, and, of course, the travel industry has never been the same since.

"You got out just in time," friends have said, but, really, there had been no strategy to my timing other than the fact that I had turned 65. I was ready to let go of the competition. Throughout life, I had lived in a perpetual state of rivalry; it was like when two guys on motorcycles meet at a traffic light and wordlessly challenge each other to a race. One guy revs his engine—*vroom, vroom!*—and the other revs his in response—*vroom, vroom, vroom!* What I had learned is that I didn't need to rev my engine all the time, only when it was warranted.

I had taken up tennis in my 40s and realized for the first time that I didn't have to win at everything. It was more important for me to play good tennis and hit the ball and enjoy myself, even if I lost.

I wanted to travel as much as ever, but now I would get to do it for me rather than for business. I also wanted more time for simple pleasures such as reading. When I was young, I'd set a goal to read the same four books every 10 years, and I hadn't been entirely successful. Even though it took me two weeks to read the 250 pages of biography introducing the book, I did manage to read *War and Peace* by Tolstoy twice. I read *The Stranger* by Sartre just once and *Nana* by Zola three times. The only one I read four times was *Père Goriot* by Honoré de Balzac.

When I read it at the university, I enjoyed the story of the young student Rastignac, who comes from the provinces and is determined to become one of the social elite. Rastignac looks out on Paris from his vantage point in the Père Lachaise Cemetery and says, "À nous deux, maintenant!" ("It's between the two of us now!") When I finished the book, I thought, "That old man wasn't very interesting. It was really about Rastignac, who set out to conquer Paris."

When I was 50, I thought, "I get it. Père Goriot was a wise old man, and Rastignac was just a young wise guy." The book didn't change—guess who did change. Excellent books can offer a different lesson every time you read them.

After 12 years together, Trish left me without warning on New Year's Day in 1990. Then and now, I saw no signs that she was going to leave. It hurt terribly, and I fell into a funk, losing 35 pounds in short order. I turned to the church for the first time in decades for a way to make sense of things. From age 21 to age 56, I had attended church maybe 10 times, just for Easter or Christmas, but starting in 1990, I became very devout and never missed a Sunday again. Paying attention to the sermons made all the difference. I had taken a 35-year hiatus before realizing that something was missing from my life—the spiritual part of it. Although I first tried the Presbyterian Church, I felt more comfortable in the Episcopal Church. It appealed to my English roots and made me feel more connected to my father and grandfather. Once I started going to church regularly, I felt whole.

While I was single, I attended the Bush family reunion in St. Louis because William H. T. Bush (whom everyone called "Bucky") was a good friend. Bucky was George Bush Sr.'s younger brother, a businessman who still lived in St. Louis. He had introduced me to George before his days as vice president, so I always knew George as "George" and Barbara as "Barbara." I didn't ever feel the need to call him "Mr. Vice President" or, later, "Mr. President."

I had once visited the vice president's residence at the U.S. Naval Observatory grounds with Bucky and a few other people. Downstairs, we listened to a marine guard playing piano in full dress uniform while we had a few drinks. Then, Bucky said, "Come on, I'll show you upstairs."

Upstairs was where the family lived—their personal bedrooms. We were halfway up the stairs when a voice called out, "Bucky! Don't take Barney up there!"

It was Barbara, and Bucky straightened up like he'd been shot between the shoulder blades. He was surely not supposed to take someone who wasn't a family member upstairs.

"Let's go back down now," he said quietly.

By the time of the family reunion, though, George had moved out of the vice president's residence and into the White House. He had become president of the United States. All of the Bush family would travel to St. Louis for the weekend, including their only sister, Nancy.

"Just for fun, Nancy could be your date for the weekend," Bucky told me. She had lost her husband about six months earlier, and I was newly single as well.

As I got ready to leave that Friday, my CFO said, "Oh, she's perfect for you! It's a marriage made in heaven."

"Why?"

"She's seven years older than you, and statistically, you'll both die the same year."

"Thanks."

At the reunion, George said to me, "Barney, I want you to know that you're dating the most intelligent of us Bush kids."

I smiled at him and said, "Mr. President, I don't think you should be quoted as saying that."

We had a fun weekend, and neither Nancy nor I really saw it as a date—it just happened to be that we were the odd ones out. At the end of it, she took both of my hands in hers and said, "Barney, you're such a nice guy. You should find a much younger woman who can take care of you when you're an old man."

Healing from my last marriage took time, but I married again, this time to a sophisticated woman named Pam who was also interested in art. My friend Peter Ueberroth, *Time*'s "Man of the Year" in 1984, introduced us. The summer of 2001, Pam and I stayed in Seattle. She liked it there. Pam was never thrilled with St. Louis, so after having lived there for 69 years, I agreed to make the move to Seattle. I had no reason to leave, but I wanted Pam to be happy. I drew up a floor plan of the house I envisioned for us, and I hired a wonderful architect named Jim Olson to design it with concrete, limestone, and marble as the main building materials.

"There should be a wall for every major work of art," I told him.

My inspiration was a modern art museum just north of Copenhagen. I wanted the house to be a collaborative project between Jim and me. I found a wonderful waterfront property in Bellevue with 220 mature trees on it and asked Jim to site the house to spare as many trees as possible. We ended up taking down only three trees.

The house would have two glass-enclosed corridors; I had wanted the longer walkway to go to the bedroom side, but I ended up with the short corridor. I did get a wonderful window in the shower, however. Once, I'd taken a trip to the Hotel Villa San Michele outside Florence with my wife and daughter, and I'd watched a thunderstorm roll in over the Tuscan Valley through a window in the shower. Ever since then, that had become an important design element to me.

When my home in St. Louis was being built, I said to the New York architect, "Do whatever my wife wants, but I have to have a window in the shower."

He considered it and said, "It's already designed. A window in the shower will ruin the look of the outside; square just doesn't fit. What do you think of round?"

"I don't care what shape it is."

"How about if I buy a chrome porthole? It would be a lot cheaper, and it would look good."

"I think it's wonderful, but you realize you've created an instantaneous myth."

"What do you mean?"

"I'm the only person who founded two cruise lines. A hundred years from now, someone will write, 'That Ebsworth was such an eccentric that he had to have a porthole in his bathroom.' That's where myths come from."

In my new home in Bellevue, the whole length of the shower would be a window that led to an alcove with a Japanese garden. It would feel like showering in the midst of nature.

Jim did a great job designing a home that was the perfect place for my art collection. Automatic blinds would ensure that direct sunlight didn't damage the paintings, and the simple design of the home ensured that the architecture didn't overshadow the art. I liked the idea of living in a home that felt like a museum. It was direct and uncluttered, qualities I wanted my life to embody.

Unfortunately, when the house was ready, Pam didn't move in. After 12 years, she told me she was leaving just a couple months before we were due to move in 2003. In retrospect, that shouldn't have been much of a surprise: she had been married and divorced four times before.

All three of the women I married were with me for 12 years and never remarried afterward, and I have remained friends with all. Feeling otherwise has never made sense to me; why invite animosity into your life? I can't say coming to terms with the end of a relationship is an easy process, but I listened to the church's teachings about love and forgiveness and knew the only reasonable way to live with myself was to move forward and appreciate the time we had together.

I could have just stayed in St. Louis, but I had already had this delightful home built and went ahead with the move anyway. The first day I stayed in my new home, I looked out the window and said to myself, "I live here." The Olympic Mountains were visible from my backyard, covered with snow nearly year-round. Quite a sight.

Moving meant changes for not only me but also my collection. Once I'd settled in and made Seattle my home, I decided that was where my art would live on, too.

Whereas I'd always planned to give my collection to the St. Louis Art Museum when I died, now I changed plans. In 2008, I announced my intention to donate the bulk of my American modernist collection to the Seattle Art Museum. I surmise that there are about 10 people who want me to come back to St. Louis and about 300 people who want the collection to come back.

Shortly after my announcement, my friend Patti Junker was lecturing during an Edward Hopper show at the museum, and she directed the audience's attention to a big movie screen. After a flick of a remote, my friend Steve Martin appeared on the screen.

"Barney, I'm sorry I couldn't be there tonight, but I'm next door having dinner," he said—and I laughed. I had no idea this was coming.

After a few opening jokes, he described how he first noticed me. "I remember when I first started collecting American modernist pictures in the early '70s; I would open books, and I would see a great O'Keeffe, and I would look and see who owned it, and it would say 'Barney Ebsworth,' or a great Stella and it would say 'Barney Ebsworth,' and I thought, 'I love this guy! He's got all the great pictures.' As I kept collecting on, I would see a great Hopper—it would say 'Barney Ebsworth'—or a great Marsden Hardley, and I thought, 'Gosh, I just *hate* this guy.' And I knew that one day, because you are a generous man, you would probably give the pictures to me. But that didn't happen. Instead, you gave them to the Seattle Art Museum, which is fine. It's fine. Not only, Barney, are you a great person to get high with, but you are also now a great philanthropist and have been for a long, long time. The people of Seattle thank you. Not only that, but the people of the United States thank you for this great, great gift. And so, Barney, I salute you."

I loved the "getting high" comment. Actually, when we were together, Steve and I never drank anything stronger than tea. I don't get high, and I suspect he doesn't, either.

Steve is much more active at selling works than I am. He frequently refreshes his collection by selling off old pieces and buying new ones. On the other hand, I didn't sell a painting until 2010, when it became a matter of practicality.

After the excitement of building my house, I was looking for another worthwhile project in my retirement. Inspired in part by Stephen Holl's Chapel of St. Ignatius at Seattle University, I decided to leave another gift to the city of Seattle that I'd grown to love: I wanted to build an Anglican chapel in a park for public meditation and community meetings. I approached leading Japanese architect Tadao Ando to design it.

"I feel bad for architects," I told him. "You can design terrific projects and they never get funded. I'm going to fund this 100 percent myself, though, so you can be assured it will get made."

It would be a significant landmark for Seattle. Pope John Paul II had invited six of the world's best architects to submit designs for a new chapel to be built in Rome to commemorate the two-thousandth anniversary of Christianity, and Ando had been one of the six, though his design wasn't ultimately chosen. It was a scaled-down version of this design that I planned to bring to Seattle. I imagined it as a beautiful, peaceful place that would draw architecture aficionados and "regular townspeople" alike.

Although a number of culturally aware people were excited by the prospect of an Ando chapel, I had my first experience with NIMBY: "not in my backyard." Residents near the site I had originally planned for it objected, citing traffic concerns. Although I explained that it would seat only 145 people and have just one religious service per week, they still didn't want it. Essentially, what they all told me was "We think this is a great idea. You should build this chapel . . . just not in my backyard." It astonished me that they would turn down this gift, but I agreed to look elsewhere.

When I found the second site—which was even better, ensconced in a beautiful park on Capitol Hill—I paid $6 million for the land and hired a public relations firm to talk to the neighbors. The firm organized three community meetings and, in effect, organized the opposition. A local lawyer wanted to ambulance chase and charge his neighbors to stop me from building the chapel. The PR firm did nothing but throw gasoline on the fire, and the community this time was not just disapproving but also oddly angry. One less than honorable newspaper reporter ran a long article questioning my motives and quoting people who called the project a "vanity temple" for a "rich guy from Hunts Point." Presumably, he ran the harshest quotes he could find because I had not agreed to speak with him for his article. Journalists are not among my favorite people.

What used to be an honorable profession to promote your city and uncover corruption has become an opportunity to self-promote—and to hell with the city. In fact, this journalist was doing something detrimental to the community by helping to drive me out of town. I find it very distressing.

Finally, one of the residents near my original site contacted the city council and asked, "Why don't you help find a place for this man?"

The council agreed. Bellevue city officials helped me scout other locations while I worked out the funding, now for the third time. Originally, I had planned to sell my Build-A-Bear Workshop stock to fund the chapel. In May, the stocks were worth $30 a share, and I had two million shares—that would mean $60 million. Of that, I planned for $15 million to go to build Christiane a home, $30 million for the church, and $15 million for the endowment to run it.

However, just before I sold my shares, the board announced that Maxine was going to sell the company.

"Well, then, I'll wait," I said. "I came into this business with Maxine, and nothing would make me happier than for us to go out together."

By October, we had three buyers interested, but because of the recession, suddenly nobody could borrow enough money. We were unable to sell, and the stock collapsed. I sold all my shares for about $9 million instead of $60 million. It would not be enough to fund the chapel.

The idea still gnawed at me, though. I had to find an alternate way to get it done. In church, an idea hit: *They just sold a Warhol for $76 million. It's nowhere near as good as mine. I'll sell the Warhol and build the chapel.*

I contracted with Christie's to sell Andy Warhol's *Big Campbell Soup Can with Can Opener (Vegetable)* in its November 2010 auction. It was an iconic early painting of Warhol's and sure to draw a significant price. Experts bet it would sell for between $60 and $80 million.

Instead, the auction fell apart.

Christie's failed to tell me that its two competitors were featuring a major Warhol on the cover of their sales catalogs and their auctions were before my auction at Christie's. Christie's also failed to tell me that it had already promised the cover of its main catalog to another collector. Although Christie's had produced a 120-page private catalog about just my picture, it came out four days before the auction and few saw it. The picture sold for $22 million, far below the low estimate. Had I known, I would not have sold it.

That was the last sign for me that the chapel wasn't meant to be. I don't suspect the idea will be resuscitated. After fighting for it for so many years, I grew weary of the hurdles and opposition. It was the antithesis of what I was offering, which was supposed to be a place of peace for the community.

I have found satisfaction in other projects and other ways to honor my family. My St. Louis church, the Church of St. Michael and St. George, provides housing for low-income families. Originally, the program operated similarly to Habitat for Humanity and built homes called St. Michael's Houses for people who otherwise wouldn't be able to afford to own homes. In 1998, I donated a St. Michael's House in memory of my father, Alec W. Ebsworth.

When I told my sister what I'd done, she simply asked, "What about Mom?"

Naturally, I then had to donate another one in memory of my mother, Bernice W. Ebsworth, in 1999. In 2001, I made a $1 million donation in memory of my parents to save and restore the Frank Lloyd Wright House in Kirkwood, Missouri. It had been built in 1955 and would be preserved as a house museum with the original furnishings and fabrics, open for docent-led private tours. It was one of only five Wright houses in the state and is now on the National Register of Historic Places. Wright called it a "Usonian" house, an abbreviated version of "United States." Because of my donation, the property it stands on is now called Ebsworth Park.

The "project" that's meant the most to me, however, is becoming a grandfather. My daughter met Mark Ladd through a mutual friend, and I liked him from the moment I met him. He seemed like a fine young man, and once I met his family, I liked them as well. They're very genuine.

I was excited to hear that this was the man she would marry. I gave my daughter an unlimited budget for her wedding, and she exceeded it. About 300 people attended the reception at the Chicago Club, and the manager told me he'd never seen the place look better in 25 years.

"There isn't a single red rose left in Chicago this weekend," he said.

The following day, people called to tell me how wonderful the reception was, and several people mentioned that they really enjoyed the band. Most of them didn't realize that there were actually two bands—the place was so large that two bands were hired for different rooms, and many people never even made it to the other room.

Alexandra was their first child, and Maximilian was their second. She's a dramatic Sarah Bernhardt type and a scamp. He's a sweet little boy and on the quieter side. The only thing better than children is grandchildren. You can play with them and wind them up and then give them back.

They have two great parents and are being reared the right way, with love and discipline. Our agreement is that Christiane brings the kids to my home for a week in the summer, and then she picks a place—usually warm—for winter vacation for all of us.

Whenever I travel in their direction, I also stop in to see them for a couple of days. My greatest joys are my daughter and my grandkids.

Although I'm sure she could have done a fine job with it, I never planned to leave my business to Christiane because I wanted her to enjoy her life. I feel good that I'm able to help support her so she can do what she loves most: be a mother to her children.

There's a saying that when you retire, you start dying. Not me. I'm enjoying my retirement just as I've enjoyed every other part of my life. Like most other things, I think it's a matter of perspective—the more you can look around and appreciate what you have at any stage, the better your life will be. The list of things to love about this world is limitless, from the flawless gifts of nature to the flawed and fascinating people around us. How lucky we are.

Afterword

I've always had a mind like a steel trap—and I still do, except it's rusting, which is why I began writing down my memories. When I decided to work on a book, it was above all for my daughter, Christiane.

I remember when I was just starting out in the travel industry and sitting with Harry Pope, who ran the Food Service Management Guild. About 10 years later, I ran into him again, and we were both driving Rolls-Royces.

"Who would have thought that you and I would both be driving Rolls-Royces?" Harry asked.

"I always knew you'd be driving one," I said. "It's me I didn't expect!"

If I had to pinpoint the qualities that made me successful in business, I'd list them as my tendency to stay ahead of the curve and reinvent the business as needed, my willingness to pay more to hire the best workers, my ability to put myself in my customers' shoes and figure out what they wanted, and my skills as a problem solver.

I think many businesspeople get mired in their early successes and believe they can make the same business model work forever. It's just not so, especially in today's smartphone- and Internet-driven world. If you're not reinventing yourself, something is probably wrong.

The quality that made me successful at *life* was even simpler: a positive attitude. I've kept my positive attitude, in part, by surrounding myself with people and things that make me happy. That doesn't mean I forget about the world's misfortunes; I donate to the United Way and Salvation Army because I know they do very good work for people in need. Every few years, the Salvation Army invites me to come to a meeting and join the board, but I can't stomach it. Luckily for me, the organization needs my money more than it needs my time as a volunteer; I'd much rather send checks every year and not have to witness the day-to-day challenges it faces, though I admire it greatly for the deeds it does. I worked hard to get out of economic danger, and I find it very depressing to see families struggling to get by.

For my own family, I just want them to stay happy and healthy. I want my grandkids to get a great education and my daughter and son-in-law to continue to have a loving marriage—and I feel confident that all of those things will happen.

Although I'm reasonably sure I'm not going to get out of this world alive, I don't spend much time thinking about death or what will happen afterward. It's not something that scares me. I'm already living in heaven—I think heaven and hell are right here on earth and we decide which one we live in. But whatever comes after death, I'm sure it will be all right.

I'd like to be remembered as an honest, hardworking, reasonably intelligent, and loving man. From my father, I learned the importance of being fair, and I pass that same lesson on to my daughter and grandkids. I hope they will always know how much they have enriched my life and that I have lived with no regrets. Truly, it is a wonderful life.